ROOM 606

The SAS House and the Work of Arne Jacobsen

Michael Sheridan

ROOM 606

The SAS House and the Work of Arne Jacobsen

This book reconstructs a building that no longer truly exists so that we may rediscover a lost world of form and sensation and gain a deeper understanding of the work of Arne Jacobsen. While best known beyond his native Denmark as a furniture designer, Jacobsen was one of the outstanding architects of the twentieth century, and the artistic and cultural value of his work has only increased in the years since his death.

The building is the SAS House, a high-rise hotel and airline terminal completed in Copenhagen for the Scandinavian Airlines System, SAS, in 1960. It was Jacobsen's masterwork, a project that condensed the architectural strategies and formal preoccupations of a lifetime into a single setting. Throughout his career, Jacobsen attempted to create complete environments, buildings in which the exterior and interior, furnishings, and finishes were melded into an integrated whole. The SAS House was the pinnacle of these efforts. By the time the project was finished, he had completed his building with new types of furniture, lighting, textiles, and objects.

Tragically, the SAS House has been reduced to a virtual shell. The building still contains a hotel and airline offices, but while the exterior is intact, the distinctive interiors and unique fixtures—integral parts of Jacobsen's work—have been discarded or altered beyond recognition. Of the SAS House's 275 guest rooms, only one, Room 606, remains relatively untouched, retaining the built-in woodwork, custom fabrics, and unique palette of colors Jacobsen created for all the Royal Hotel's guest rooms. Examined in detail, Room 606 allows us to reconstruct the SAS House and trace the underlying themes of Jacobsen's career.

The primary instruments of this reconstruction are some 120 photos taken shortly after the building was completed by Aage Strüwing, an architectural photographer who collaborated with Jacobsen from the late 1930s through the early 1960s. The thousands of drawings and sketches that Jacobsen and his staff produced during the design process also provide insight into the development of the SAS House. To underscore the contemporary nature of Room 606, architectural photographer Paul Warchol has created a series of new images especially for this book. His pictures capture Jacobsen's masterful use of color and form.

Until very recently, serious examination of Jacobsen's work was virtually nonexistent. Between 1964, when Tobias Faber's monograph was published, and 1997, most of the literature on Jacobsen consisted of magazine articles and small exhibition catalogues. Only a handful of serious documents were produced. In the early 1990s, Felix Solaguren-Bescoa published a guidebook to Jacobsen's buildings as well as compilations of drawings and photos that hinted at the richness and complexity of the work. Poul Erik Tøjner and Kjeld Vindum's 1994 book *Arne Jacobsen: Architect and Designer* gathered interviews with many of Jacobsen's colleagues and associates into an important work of oral history. The need for a complete survey of Jacobsen's career was finally answered in 1998 by Carsten Thau and Kjeld Vindum. Their comprehensive work, *Arne Jacobsen*, is, and will certainly remain, the definitive survey of Jacobsen's vast and varied output. While this book is indebted to these previous works, it is an altogether different undertaking.

Jacobsen's focus on a few primary themes produced buildings in which the parts were condensed versions of the whole. The SAS House distilled these themes into an encyclopedic array of architecture, furniture, and the applied arts. Based on the idea of the room as microcosm, the book is divided into chapters that examine Room 606 from several angles and trace the relationships between the room and the building, then traces the origins of the SAS House in a series of earlier works as well as its influence on later work, closing the circle between Room 606 and Jacobsen's prolific production. The first two chapters explore the development of the SAS House and its status an as abstract equivalent to the natural world that captivated Jacobsen and provided the underlying theme of his work. The central portion of the book uses Room 606 as a means to reconstruct the SAS House from exterior to interior, in a vertical journey that culminates in the hotel guest rooms. The final chapters examine the array of smaller works and objects Jacobsen created for the building and which manifested his themes at the scale of the human body.

By necessity, a number of exemplary buildings are mentioned only in passing or omitted entirely. For a complete accounting of Jacobsen's production, the interested reader is directed to Thau and Vindum's magnum opus. Nonetheless, it is my hope that readers from a wide range of backgrounds and interests will find this book offers a worthwhile perspective on one of the great talents of modernism and his most complete creation.

Room 606 is not a time capsule. Visitors to Copenhagen can still stay there, renting the room by the night as they would any other. Experienced as overnight accommodation, the room provides thrirty square meters of elegant surfaces and understated luxury. Examined in the context of Jacobsen's vanished masterpiece, it provides entry into a much larger setting, a world of sensuous utility and industrial craft that is essentially timeless and utterly contemporary.

↑

Room 606, Royal Hotel, SAS House, Copenhagen, 1955–60. Jacobsen's own slide, taken shortly after the hotel opened, captures the elegant ensemble of colors, materials, and forms that he created to accommodate the guests of the Royal Hotel. The hotel rooms encapsulated the architectural themes of the twenty-two-story building and, by extension, the underlying themes of Jacobsen's long and prolific career.

In the center of Copenhagen, on the sixth floor of the SAS Royal Hotel, a single room preserves in microcosm the definitive masterwork of Arne Jacobsen. Room 606 is the last surviving interior of the SAS House, a lost world of abstract form and natural experience that was an unparalleled example of twentieth-century Scandinavian architecture and design. Completed in 1960 for the Scandinavian Airline System, the SAS House was a combination of airline terminal and luxury hotel that offered the new tourist market a seamless combination of transport and accommodation in the airline's northern hub. This monumental building also provided Jacobsen with the opportunity to exercise the full range of the talents that have distinguished him as one of the twentieth century's most complex and versatile architects. He designed every detail of the building and the interiors, from the twenty-two-story hotel tower to furniture, lighting, and textiles to the flatware for the hotel restaurant.

The result was a modern *Gesamtkunstwerk*, a total work of art, that condensed the architectural strategies and formal preoccupations of a lifetime into a single setting. Although Jacobsen designed it in the late 1950s, the SAS House reflected themes that dated back to the 1920s and, in the case of his preoccupation with cultivated nature, to the architect's boyhood. Challenged by a project whose size and variety of functions were unprecedented in his experience, Jacobsen gathered and transformed the primary themes of his career into a complete environment. The SAS House was also a turning point in Jacobsen's work and served as the foundation for the final phase of his long career. Following its completion in 1960, he would produce a series of buildings, projects, and objects that continued to develop his unique synthesis of abstraction and naturalism, including St. Catherine's College at Oxford (1960–64) and the National Bank of Denmark (1961–78).

The cultural value of Room 606 is not as a time capsule—the room is still rented by the night—but as the key to a body of work that embraced the contradictions of Jacobsen's time, and our own. The guest rooms of the Royal Hotel condensed the formal themes of the SAS House into a single chamber. Jacobsen's furniture, lighting, and textiles were designed to join beauty and utility in a single integrated setting. Room 606 contains a wealth of these artifacts, allowing us to trace the relationships between Jacobsen's architecture and his work in the applied arts. Examined in the context of the original building, Room 606 can be seen as a condensed version of the SAS House and, by extension, a portal into Jacobsen's long career.

On 1 August 1946, the chairmen of the national airlines of Denmark, Norway, and Sweden, sequestered in an Oslo hotel suite, signed an agreement establishing the Scandinavian Airlines System, SAS, a joint airline for intercontinental operations. Six weeks later, the first flight to New York, a DC-4 Skymaster christened Dan Viking, left Stockholm carrying twenty-eight passengers. Stopping in Copenhagen, and in Scotland and Newfoundland for fuel, Dan Viking arrived at La Guardia Airport twenty-five hours after takeoff. The addition of service to the American West

Postcard for the Scandinavian Airlines
System, 1951. SAS was created through
a merger of the national airlines of
Denmark, Sweden and Norway. All three
countries were governed by constitutional
monarchies, and royal iconography was
used to emphasize Scandinavia's common
culture. This early promotional postcard
features stamps bearing the portraits of
the three kings and the airline logo, a
combination of the heraldic shields and
flags of the member nations.

Promotional postcards, 1950–54. Stylized
versions of the Viking longboat, complete
with dragon head, were painted on the air-
craft to underscore the navigational
prowess of Scandinavian pilots in both
ancient and modern times.

Advertising materials for the SAS Polar
Route, 1954. Royal Viking service to North
America used advanced navigational
equipment to fly over the North Pole, cut-
ting travel time from twenty-seven to sixteen hours and allowing direct flights from
Copenhagen to Los Angeles. The resulting
influx of American tourists convinced SAS
that Copenhagen would require a modern,
first-class hotel, and the airline soon
began planning for the SAS House.

Coast eight years later, and the increased speed of the DC-8 jet then in development, provided SAS with a complex set of opportunities and challenges. By 1956, its marketing department was projecting an imminent invasion of tourists to Scandinavia, largely from the United States. They believed it was imperative that Copenhagen provide a modern hotel with the comforts and amenities North Americans expected.

SAS essentially decided to construct a Grand Hotel for the Jet Age, a contemporary equivalent to the cosmopolitan palaces of the prewar era, such as the Ritz in Paris and the Waldorf-Astoria in New York. To construct the new building, the airline created a subsidiary company, SAS Investa A/S, which would build and manage this hotel in Copenhagen and, eventually, a string of hotels throughout the world. The airline planned to combine a hotel for tourists with an air terminal that would shuttle travelers to and from Kastrup Airport, twenty kilometers to the south, via a fleet of special buses. The new SAS House would allow the airline to consolidate all aspects of its operations in a single location, but it would require a central location, convenient for residents and close to the major tourist attractions.

The founding of København, the "merchants' harbor," is generally credited to Absalon, the Bishop of Roskilde, who constructed a fortress on an island between the harbor and a fishing village in 1167. As the village grew into a city, it expanded in a series of concentric rings, protected by castellated ramparts and moats. In the 1800s, new institutions that could not be accommodated in the medieval core were located at the edge of the city, beyond the walls. In 1843, writer-architect Georg Carstensen founded the world's first permanent public amusement park and beer garden, the Tivoli Gardens, along Vesterbrogade, the road leading out from the western gate of the city. The first railroad station in Denmark, serving the line between Copenhagen and Roskilde, was erected in 1817 a few blocks farther west. Both Tivoli Gardens and the train station expanded with the growth of the rail network and the working class.

Diagonally along Vesterbrogade from the Tivoli Gardens, by then the most popular attraction in Copenhagen, lay an empty wedge of property abutting the railroad's trench. In spite of its prime location, the site was generally considered unbuildable and had accommodated an open-air market for decades. The city government had long sought development of the triangular property, so much so that the terms of sale to a private developer after World War II stipulated that as long as the site remained vacant, any profit realized by its resale would revert to the public treasury. Under these circumstances, SAS was able to arrange an eighty-year lease for an initial rent of six million Danish kroner per year, a relative bargain at the time.

Prior to the selection of an architect, the airline had hired the engineering and construction firm Kampsax A/S to prepare a feasibility study. A trio of ink drawings, dated 1955, illustrate the organization of the project. A drawing of the building facade along Vesterbrogade establishes the basic scheme of a two-story building with a hotel tower above. In the south elevation, a

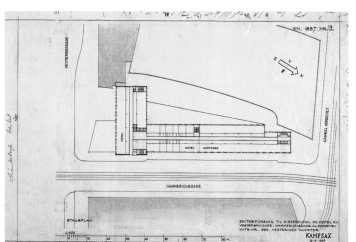

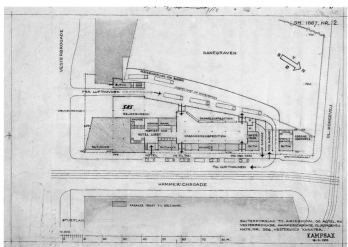

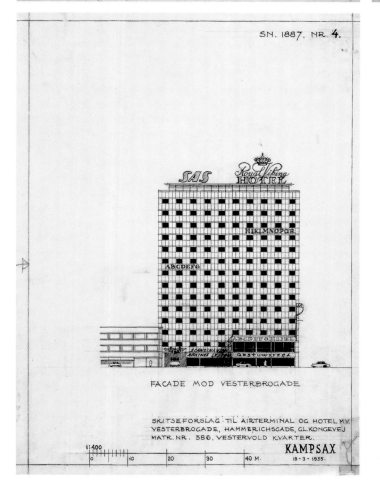

Schematic designs by Kampax A/S, SAS House, march 1955. After locating a vacant site in the center of Copenhagen, SAS hired Kampsax A/S, one of the leading Danish construction and engineering companies, to draw a plan for a building that combined a hotel with a satellite passenger terminal. The trian-gular site next to the open trench of the railroad tracks resulted in a pair of narrow volumes arranged at a right angle parallel to the street frontages. This set of ink drawings depict an L-shaped slab with hotel rooms atop a ground floor filled with airline functions. Bus service to and from the airport would be routed from Vesterbrogade to the edge of the trench, before exiting onto Hammerichsgade.

fourteen-story tower with a recessed penthouse displays advertising on its facade and is crowned by neon signs for the airline and the Royal Hotel, which resemble the neon-lit facades of the buildings on the Town Hall Square, two blocks to the east. The second-floor plan illustrates a podium extending the length of Hammerichsgade, filled with hotel rooms that share elevators with the tower. A ground-floor plan depicts the bus traffic from the airport entering the site from Vesterbrogade, serving the air terminal at the north end of the site, and exiting on the side street, Hammerichsgade. The hotel lobby is located between the air terminal and a deep block of retail space extending to Vesterbrogade.

In 1955, Jacobsen was fifty-three years old and approaching the summit of his career. Since the beginning of the decade, he had designed and constructed a series of buildings that had brought him international recognition and confirmed his place in the firmament of modern architecture. Among these works were the Søholm row houses, the A. Jespersen and Sons office building (which would serve as the prototype of the SAS House tower), and the Rødovre Town Hall. The architect's beloved Munkegård School was finally under construction, and he had recently been invited to participate in the Hansaviertel Interbau housing exhibition, along with Alvar Aalto, Le Corbusier, and Jacobsen's former professor Kay Fisker. The following year, he would be appointed as a professor of architecture at his alma mater, the Royal Danish Academy of Fine Arts, the ultimate sign of acceptance within the parochial Danish architectural establishment.

It is difficult to imagine an architect better suited to design the SAS House than Jacobsen. Over the previous thirty years, he had designed a wide range of buildings that prepared him for the air terminal and hotel's complex mix of functions. The creation of dozens of single-family homes and apartment buildings had imbued his work with a profound domesticity that would permeate the hotel and result in a revolutionary rethinking of the guest rooms. In designing an array of public buildings, from athletic facilities to the town halls that were a mainstay of his practice, Jacobsen had honed his ability to devise efficient patterns of circulation for large numbers of people and to arrange complex sets of public and non public functions. His industrial work, which included laboratories and factories for the Novo pharmaceuticals company and a refinery for Maersk, had prepared him to accommodate the vast infrastructure and mechanical systems that would serve the "city within the city," as the SAS House was christened after its opening. And in the field of applied arts, Jacobsen had continued the Scandinavian tradition of designing custom furnishings for his large-scale buildings, continually developing new designs for lighting, textiles, and seating, such as the seminal Ant chair and its successor, the Seven.

In spite of his professional success and institutional acceptance, Jacobsen remained committed to the path of innovation that had made him the most controversial architect in Denmark. Since his student days at the academy, where he was schooled in an austere version of

↑
SAS publicity photo; from left to right:
Viggo Rasmussen, Danish director of SAS,
Arne Jacobsen, and Alberto Kappenberger,
hotel consultant and later general
manager of the Royal Hotel. Following a
review of the Kampsax scheme, the airline
hired Arne Jacobsen to design the flagship
building. In this photo from 1957, the three
men involved in the development of the
project survey a model of the building.
The model emphasizes the contrasting
surfaces of base and tower, as well as the
horizontal layering of the low building.

neoclassicism, Jacobsen had looked beyond the confines of Danish architectural culture for new ideas. In the late 1920s, he had found inspiration in the work of Le Corbusier; his Bellavista apartment complex (1931–34), overlooking the sound north of Copenhagen, marked the arrival of modern architecture in Denmark. In the following decade, Jacobsen found his formative model in the work of the Swedish architect Erik Gunnar Asplund.

Public acceptance of modern architecture in Denmark did not come easily. Jacobsen's six-story Stelling House, constructed for an art supply company on an ancient square in central Copenhagen, was a carefully calibrated response to a sensitive site. After its completion in 1938, however, a local newspaper suggested that he be legally prevented from building in Copenhagen again. Controversy also attended his competition-winning schemes for town halls in Aarhus and Glostrup as well as for the Munkegård School. And in the early 1950s, as he began to employ the glass curtain walls that would culminate in the pellucid skin of the SAS House, his scheme for the Glostrup Town Hall was nearly derailed by furor over the exterior cladding. Rather than being deterred by these controversies, Jacobsen continued to use whatever new technology and formal devices served his aesthetic agenda.

Regardless of his controversial past—and perhaps partly because of it—SAS selected Jacobsen to design their landmark in the summer of 1955. In retrospect, the commission seems to have been another aspect of the airline's strategy of using Scandinavian culture as a marketing tool. Beyond his international reputation, Jacobsen's ability to work within a budget for a broad range of public and private clients must have provided reassurance to SAS's board of directors. While it was anticipated that the SAS House would be Jacobsen's most complete work, no one could have anticipated that it would also be the most controversial.

Over the next five years, Jacobsen's architectural office, or *tegnestue*, drawing office, as it is known in Denmark, produced thousands of sketches and drawings that examined and detailed every aspect of the monumental project and its interiors. Jacobsen began his work with a series of three-dimensional block studies, variations on Kampsax's scheme, that evaluated different configurations of tower and podium on the basis of room sizes and usable square footage. By the end of September 1955, these efforts had confirmed the basic scheme of a double-loaded hotel tower, set back from Vesterbrogade and positioned at a right angle to a two-story podium containing the public areas.

From the first announcement of the airline's intentions, the SAS House was surrounded by controversy. The initial round of criticism centered on the bus traffic that would serve the air terminal and, critics feared, cause further congestion at the intersection of Vesterbrogade and Hammerichsgade, one of the busiest in the city. Jacobsen's studies of massing and circulation naturally included this bus traffic, and he quickly proposed constructing a platform over the adjacent rail trench that would provide a parking lot and allow the buses access to the air terminal

↑ ↑

Bellavista Apartments, Klampenborg, 1931–34. This set of austere white buildings introduced modernism to Denmark. Behind the rounded corners and abstract surfaces that were inspired by the work of Le Corbusier, ingenious planning provided each apartment with a balcony and a view of the sea. The site plan of staggered forms around a central court established a planning device that Jacobsen would develop for the rest of his career.

↖

Aarhus Town Hall, Aarhus, 1937–42. Aarhus town hall was Jacobsen's first major public building and the first of many controversial episodes in his career. Critics who demanded a more "dignified" material attacked the original design of smooth plaster surfaces, and the building was finally clad in gray marble from western Norway. Others insisted that a town hall required a tower, and the town council compelled Jacobsen and his partner, Erik Møller, to add a skeletal framework.

↑

Søllerød Town Hall, Søllerød, 1939–42. This pair of offset volumes was covered in Porsgruun marble with low roofs of copper. The town hall was one of Jacobsen's prewar triumphs and still retains the full range of finishes, woodwork, and accessories that he and his partner Flemming Lassen designed to meet all the inhabitants' needs.

from Vesterport, along the north edge of the site. While the engineering required to construct the platform would add substantially to the construction costs, it effectively answered the critics. From Jacobsen's perspective, it also created a straight path from sidewalk to parking lot for the passengers, and it allowed him to design a rectangular podium, rather than an irregular wedge, that would provide a regular base for the hotel tower.

The first montage released for publication illustrates this "square" and serves as evidence of Jacobsen's affinity for classical planning devices, which would reappear in the lower floors of the final project. To provide an appropriate sense of enclosure, Jacobsen extended the airline terminal along Vesterport with an enormous gateway to allow the buses to enter the site. (The airline evidently found the additional floor space unnecessary, and the extension was deleted from the project.) Along Vesterbrogade, at the difficult intersection between the tower and the neighboring three-story commercial building, a smaller passage allowed buses to exit directly onto the boulevard. The connection with the adjacent building would eventually be resolved by recessing the podium, creating a slot that extended the shops of the hotel and served pedestrians. Construction began in the summer of 1956 with the platform over the trench, though Jacobsen and the contractor continued to develop the design of the building. By October, the first stage of the platform was supported by piers set between the tracks, and the site had been cleared for excavation and foundation work.

The SAS House was constructed of reinforced concrete, cast on-site in wooden forms, one floor at a time. While Jacobsen had previously used precast concrete for its smooth surface and dimensional accuracy, it would have added considerably to the building cost. To cover the rough texture of site-cast concrete, Jacobsen clad the structure with stone, wood, and glass that reflected his aesthetic of suspended pattern. While the lower floors, the two-story podium, and the basements were constructed of columns and beams, the hotel tower would require a completely separate structure. To avoid columns that would intrude on the hotel rooms, where space was at a premium, or rise along the exterior walls, where the views were paramount, the tower was built as a three-dimensional framework of concrete walls. While this limited the possibility of renovations in the future—all the walls are structural—it allowed the walls to be as thin as possible. The scheme also had the advantage of limiting the transmission of sound between the rooms. The entire tower was supported on three pairs of enormous piers that penetrated the podium and continued down to bedrock. On the north side of the tower, a continuous shaft held banks of passenger elevators and service areas and contained a ventilation shaft that extended the height of the tower.

In the spring of 1958, the final images and model of the building were published internationally and were loudly condemned by local newspapers. By June, the airline had begun bus service to the airport, operating out of a temporary facility in the parking lot. That same month, a press release announced the scale and ambitions of the new building:

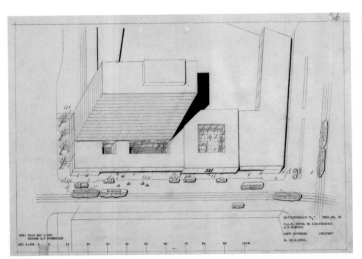

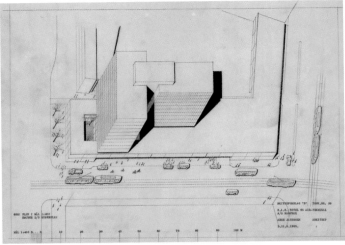

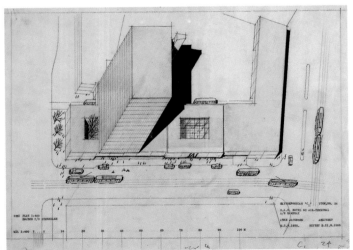

Three-dimensional studies, SAS House, August/September 1955. Jacobsen began his work on the SAS House by preparing a series of studies that investigated different arrangements of the slab and base established by the Kampsax study. All of these schemes are predicated on the construction of a platform, the *banegraven*, over the rail trench in order to create the "SAS Square" for parking and bus service. At the back of the site, a low wing extends along Vesterfarmigsgade to provide spatial definition.

A 22-floor "skyscraper" hotel and air terminal—first of its kind in Europe—is being built in Copenhagen by Scandinavian Airlines System for the age of jet travel. It is scheduled to open in 1960, when SAS will be serving the European "Gay Gateway" city with medium-range Caravelle and long-range DC-8 jet airliners [...]

The SAS hotel-terminal—dominating the center of the Danish capital—is expected to cost 30 million Danish crowns ($4,300,000). It will be the largest hotel in Scandinavia. The ultra-modern "skyscraper" will consist of three major, integrated units:
- the hotel, itself, which will be called the "Royal Hotel".
- a ticket and passenger terminal, equipped with Europe's first jet-speed "electronic brain" reservations system. The terminal may be completed by October of this year.
- a complete service station, with parking space for 300 cars.

The square-shaped foundation of the building will consist of four floors—two above ground, two below. The lobby of the hotel, the air terminal, ladies and gentlemen's hairdressers, a nursery and related facilities will be housed on these two floors. On top of the foundation, but set back from the sides, will be the hotel itself—rising 18 floors above Copenhagen. The foundation floors will be plated with a dark gray-green enamel. The hotel stories will be dominantly glass, in a lighter shade of gray-green—a giant mirror to reflect the sky and the drifting clouds. . . .

The SAS Royal Hotel will have 275 rooms, with a total of 475 beds. Each room will have a private bath, telephone, radio and television outlet. The entire building will be air-conditioned. The hotel will feature special drawing rooms and lounges for private parties, a distinctive snack bar, a large restaurant, and two cocktail bars [...]

The spacious hotel lobby—covering an area of 700 square meters—will house a large collection of quality shops. Products sold will range from furs and leather to porcelain and silver. The lobby will connect directly with the new SAS ticket and passenger terminal. The terminal will contain an air travel bureau, a bank, a car hire service, and a cocktail bar [...]

"SAS Square"—just outside the hotel-terminal building—will offer motorists a "Jet-Service" Station, with parking space for 100 cars. An underground garage, connected with the service station by a sloping ramp, will accommodate another 200 cars. The SAS "skyscraper" has been designed by architect Arne Jacobsen, Professor of the Academy of Arts, Copenhagen [...]

Four months later, the "Formes Scandinaves" exhibition, a show of Nordic design at the Musée des Arts Décoratifs in Paris, featured a full-scale prototype of a Royal Hotel guest room, designed by Jacobsen with his characteristic attention to composition and lighting. Along one wall, wall-hung cabinets were converted into glass showcases for the flatware and assorted objects he had designed for the hotel. On the opposite wall, a bed was covered with woven fabrics of his own design. The centerpiece of the tableau was an enormous photo of the two-meter-high model

↑
SAS House site, August 1957. Once the platform over the rail trench was completed, excavations for the building began. In the background, diagonally across the intersection, the entry pavilion to Tivoli Gardens frames the trees that tower over the amusement park.

↑
Air terminal structure and temporary bus terminal, June 1958. When the structure of the air terminal was completed, SAS constructed a temporary building and initiated bus service to the airport in an attempt to accustom travelers to the new routine.
In the background, the rising tower of the Royal Hotel obscures the view of Tivoli.

↓
Royal Hotel tower, January 1959. When the concrete frame of the hotel tower was completed, a ceremony was held on the roof of the building, which was then crowned with flags.

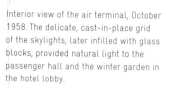

Interior view of the air terminal, October 1958. The delicate, cast-in-place grid of the skylights, later infilled with glass blocks, provided natural light to the passenger hall and the winter garden in the hotel lobby.

Royal Hotel tower, February 1959. The structure of the hotel tower consisted of reinforced concrete trays and interior walls that provided structural stability against wind loading. The curtain wall was constructed of slender aluminum bars that were bolted to the concrete parapet walls.

Jacobsen and Rasmussen inspecting one of the Royal Hotel rooms, January 1959. In the background, the tower of the Town Hall and a group of church steeples punctuate the six-story fabric of central Copenhagen.

Royal Hotel tower, July 1959. The tower was glazed from the top down. This view from Vesterbrogade illustrates the transparent corners that were critical to Jacobsen's conception of a luminous volume set above a dark base.

← Aerial view of the SAS House, 1960. The SAS House was constructed amid, and atop, the infrastructure of modern Copenhagen. To the left is Poul Baumann's Vesterport office complex, whose curves followed those of the rail trench. To the lower left, Heinrich Wenck's central rail station sits atop the tracks that followed the old city walls, demolished at the end of the nineteenth century. To the lower right, across Hammerichsgade, are Tivoli Gardens.

↓ "Formes Scandinaves" exhibition, Musée des Arts Décoratifs, Paris, 1958. Jacobsen used the exhibition to unveil his designs for the Royal Hotel guest rooms and furniture, including the Egg and Swan chairs. A section of wenge paneling lit by wall and floor lamps from the Visor series was hung with vitrines to display his new flatware. The center installation showcased an enormous photograph of the model of the SAS House, complete with clouds and subtle reflections.

of the SAS House that had been constructed for publication. It was, in the words of a writer for *Dansk Kunsthaandværk*, the magazine of the applied arts, a "one-man show." By the end of the year, the tower structure was completed. On 3 January 1959, a small celebration was held at the summit. After more than three years of careful design work, Jacobsen had finalized the exterior cladding, and the glazing of the tower could begin. Construction proceeded at a rapid pace, and the air terminal was opened in August; the Royal Hotel would follow the next July.

CHAPTER 1
TERRAIN

↑
Room 606, Royal Hotel, SAS House,
Copenhagen, 1955–1960. The last of the
original hotel rooms preserves the built-in
wood paneling that creates a base for the
light walls and the band of windows overlooking the city. The horizontal layering of
materials and views creates the sense of
enclosure and expansion equivalent to a
classical landscape.

Jacobsen's abstract forms were grounded in a deep appreciation of the natural world, and the synthesis of architecture and horticulture was the foundation of his lifework. His earliest use of nature as a wellspring for creativity was the watercolors of plants and landscapes that he painted as a child, the legacy of an artistic mother who practiced botanical illustration. The creation of apparent depth on a two-dimensional surface would remain with Jacobsen for the rest of his life and influenced both his architecture and his work in the applied arts. As an adult, he became an obsessive and skilled gardener, both personally and professionally, using his garden as a laboratory for color and texture. The SAS House was filled with episodes of a distilled nature, rooms in which natural materials were subjected to modular principles and light and texture were used to evoke the lush tactility of a garden.

In Room 606, Jacobsen's experience as a painter is evident in the use of contrasting colors and materials to create a sense of implied depth on the bedroom walls. The room is ringed with a continuous band of wenge, an African hardwood, that protects the walls from the furniture and supports a series of built-in tables. Above the paneling, the inner walls are covered in a textured fabric that is painted a watery shade of green. Below the paneling, a wood baseboard is painted a light gray that harmonizes with the dappled gray carpet and creates the effect of a shallow tray of space. The light shades of gray and green suggest a continuous surface, but the effect of continuity is interrupted by the dark color and rich pattern of the wenge that projects into the room, separating the light colors and pushing them into the background. The result is an artificial horizon, which splits the wall into foreground and background, reminiscent of the open countryside.

The woodwork continues along the outer wall of the room, where the sensation of depth becomes literal with the band of

↑
Room 606. Panels of subtle wood grain wrap around the room, serving as a head-board for the twin beds and supporting the cantilevered nightstands.

windows that offer a panoramic view over central Copenhagen. The juxtaposition of woodwork and windows produces the effect of the borrowed scenery in a Japanese print, in which a window or door frames a distant object, and, through the suppression of the middle ground, collapses the distance between the domestic and natural worlds. With the alignment of the paneling and the windows, solid walls and transparent windows form corresponding surfaces of apparent and literal depth. The result is a room that seems larger than its physical dimensions and places the guest at the center of a space that is both bounded and infinite.

→

View of the SAS House from across Vesterbrogade. The building was divided into a low two-story base containing the public areas and a twenty-story tower with 275 hotel rooms. While the tower was filled with trays of abstract landscapes, its glass skin was designed to reflect the clouds and blend into the sky.

Despite its urban location and geometric forms, the SAS House was a primary example of Jacobsen's desire for contact with the natural world, which is evident in the earliest planning stages. As he studied the arrangement of the various functions and analyzed different configurations of tower and base, Jacobsen introduced a series of courtyards that would provide natural light and focal points for the public spaces located in the low podium. The final planning study, scheme C2, included a glass-roofed hall in the air terminal and a pair of gardens that framed the hotel lobby at the base of the tower. Enclosed by walls of glass, the twin gardens would have created a transparent base for the tower. A lounge above the lobby connected the gardens, while a glass bridge leading to the hotel restaurant would have created a path through the treetops.

As the structural grid for the building developed and the detailed design process began, the early courtyards evolved into a string of top-lit halls along the central axis of the podium. In the air terminal, the glass roof became a skylight with a translucent ceiling that provided an even, diffuse light regardless of the hour. In the lobby of the Royal Hotel, the planted courtyards were combined into a two-story winter garden that continued the skylight of the passenger hall and provided a tranquil lounge adjacent to the lobby. In an early pastel sketch, the winter garden was furnished with wicker chairs and a palm tree that recalled the palm courts of nineteenth-century England, a vestige of Jacobsen's classical education in the 1920s. On the second floor of the hotel, the lounge of the early study became a vestibule that connected the restaurant with the cocktail bar and a long sitting room overlooking Hammerichsgade. The main dining room itself no longer overlooked a courtyard, but through a grid of skylights became an abstracted courtyard itself. Another early perspective sketch shows clusters of lamps covering the dining room ceiling, creating a kind of amusement-park atmosphere. In the sketch's margin, a treelike fixture with clusters of tiny bulbs resembles the lighting at Tivoli, where innumerable brightly colored lamps illuminate the gardens at night. A later pastel depicts a grid of recessed ceiling fixtures, but Jacobsen was committed to providing the dining room with natural light, and he developed a novel fixture that admitted sunlight by day and created an artificial sky at night.

In addition to the interior courtyards that provide continuous contact with the sky, Jacobsen's passion for natural effects was developed further in the building's surface treatments, textiles, and light fixtures. The lower floors of the building, for example, were lined with richly grained panels of ash, wenge, oak, and rosewood whose natural variations and colors served as a counterpoint to the extensive glass walls that lined the edges of the building and filled the floor above. While most of the veneers were cut parallel to the grain to produce an even pattern of tight, straight lines, certain areas were covered in veneers cut to expose the alternating layers of grain and fiber.

Jacobsen's use of wood as a decorative surface reached a crescendo in the air terminal, where the vibrant patterns of black-on-brown wenge that covered the walls and service

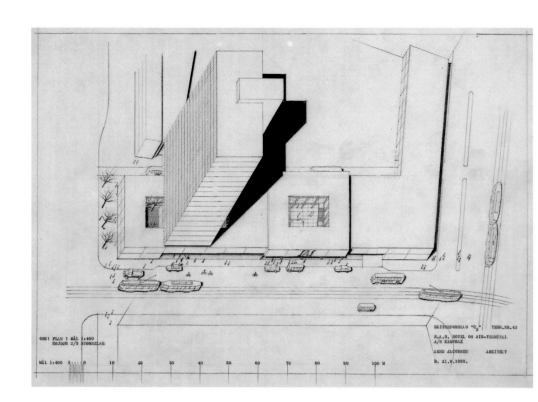

↑ ↓
Schematic plans and massing study,
variation C2, SAS House, 1956. Jacobsen's
definitive scheme was organized around
an axial arrangement of open and covered
courts. At this stage, bus traffic to the air
terminal was routed through the site to
Vesterbrogade. The two-story wing enclosing the parking lot was eliminated as the
design evolved.

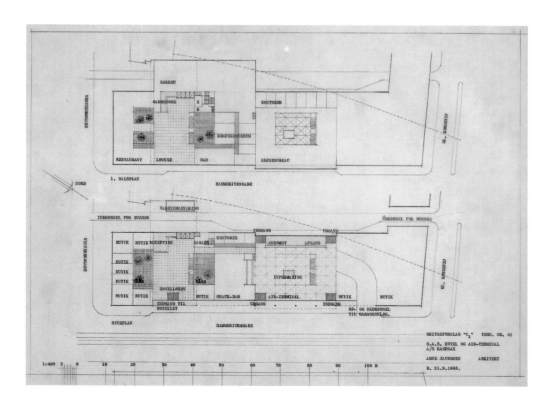

counters acted as austere corollaries to the floral wallpapers he had created in the 1940s. To complement the wood paneling, he designed carpets and curtains with subtle patterns and colors that served as geometric versions of the two-tone wood patterns. So while the walls of the second-floor lounge displayed the brown-on-brown striations of rift-cut rosewood, the floors were covered in a woven field of sea green wool with blue lines that suggested the structure of trees. This use of geometry as a counterpoint to the structure of wood and stone was reiterated on a more subtle level in the curtains Jacobsen designed to cloak the interior glass walls and to diffuse light on the second floor between the bar and restaurant.

Jacobsen designed built-in lighting fixtures that use repetition of a module to create complex spatial effects. In the Orchid Bar overlooking the winter garden, clusters of hanging lamps echoed the suspended flora in the double-paned glass walls. These simple constructions of slotted Plexiglas sheets could be used as pendants or combined into a chain of repetitive units that highlighted Jacobsen's penchant for variations on a single form. In the main dining room of the hotel restaurant, he exchanged the gridded laylight of the air terminal and the winter garden for a cluster of cylindrical skylights that blended natural and artificial light. Sixteen round openings set within the thickness of the roof were arranged in a square and filled with strings of gray glass bells that scattered sound and tinted the light from above. A ring of incandescent bulbs set between the glass coverings on the roof and the strings of bells provided artificial light at night and on overcast days. The overall effect was of an abstract constellation that echoed the gridded pattern of the carpet and the curtains along the walls. Beneath the illuminated grid, each table was furnished with a miniature version of the skylight, the Klokkelampe. With a trio of glass bells layered over a tubular lamp, these fixtures served as centerpieces for the tables, which were set with silver and glassware that Jacobsen designed specifically for the restaurant.

The use of geometric pattern as an equivalent of natural form at the SAS House highlights one of Jacobsen's greatest talents: his ability to derive inspiration from a variety of sources and transform it into a distinctive language of form and experience. Early in his career, even as his buildings were standard bearers for functionalist rhetoric and abstract form, Jacobsen layered interior walls with suspended bursts of flora, both actual and painted, in an attempt to bring the garden into the building. At the SAS House, Jacobsen transformed his earlier two-dimensional work into living objects even as he transformed natural materials into abstract form. He had been designing wallpapers and curtain fabrics since the mid-1940s, when he painted arrangements of flowers and scenes drawn from the forests and meadows of southern Sweden. He returned to these themes in the winter garden, where the restaurant's geometric carpet and curtains were juxtaposed with cascading pots of orchids that served as a kind of three-dimensional wallpaper and a living complement to the adjacent panels of wenge and rosewood.

↓
Klokkelampe (Bell Lamp). On each of the restaurant tables, a trio of glass bells stacked atop a forty-watt incandescent tube provided ambient light. The sketches below record Jacobsen's design process from gestural sculpture to refined abstraction.

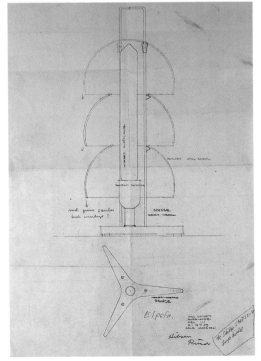

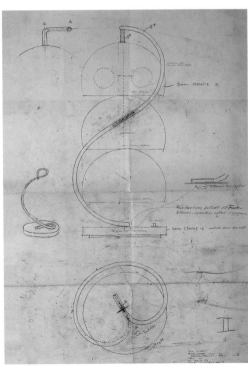

Jacobsen's minimalist aesthetic tends to obscure what was a highly romantic conception of the relationship between nature and culture. This romanticism is apparent in both his representation of his work and in his buildings. Both in the watercolors that served as his preparatory sketches and in the photographs that recorded the completed works, his buildings were shown through groups of trees, which served as both a visual frame and to locate the buildings within the natural environment. Even as his works became increasingly object like, Jacobsen continued to create interior fragments of an idealized natural world. So while his closed boxes of glass and stone from the 1950s were set in fields or otherwise isolated from their surroundings to heighten their formal power, they were filled with surfaces and interior plantings that served as connections to a larger natural context.

Like the idea of *Gesamtkunstwerk*, Jacobsen's conception of nature was a product of the nineteenth-century romantic movement, which had originated in Germany and gained cultural currency as a result of changes wrought by the Industrial Revolution. Unlike William Morris, to whom he has been compared on the basis of his textile designs, Jacobsen saw no opposition between modernity and nature. While Morris pursued a crusade against the presumed tyranny of the machine and the social systems it produced, Jacobsen devoted his energies to a more modest cause, the pursuit of beauty. In contrast to Morris and a host of earlier architects and designers who opposed the onslaught of the machine, Jacobsen did not recognize an irreconcilable gap between the natural and mechanical worlds. Instead, he embraced technology as a means of realizing his aesthetic and functional goals.

There is perhaps no more potent example of Jacobsen's use of nature as a touchstone of abstract form than the tower of the Royal Hotel. Jacobsen designed the curtain wall to blend into the sky, and his nuanced handling of proportion and color resulted in an iridescent skin that became part of the environment even as it stood apart from the surrounding buildings. The walls of the tower were covered in a grid of aluminum that was filled with planes of transparent and gray green glass. This modular structure and reflective surface signaled the curtain wall's relationship to the geometric textiles within the building and underscored the degree to which Jacobsen explored a handful of basic themes across a range of scales and materials. While his early fabric designs had used representations of plant life to bring the garden and the forest into the house, his later patterns for interior curtains and large-scale buildings joined natural experience and abstraction in a single surface.

Much of the persistent power, the oft-noted "timeless" quality of Jacobsen's mature work, stems from the complex interplay between industrial technique and natural effect. Indeed, we can discern the constant presence of nature through the entire span of his career. This presence is obvious in the early work, as the architect sculpted the landscape and opened his buildings to create overlapping vistas that connected interior and exterior. During the war years, the

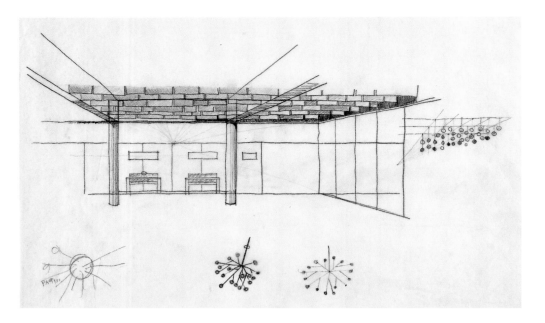

←
Sketch for lighting fixtures in the main dining room, Royal Hotel restaurant.
This early sketch of the main dining room explores the use of tiny bulbs. The light fixtures resemble abstract bushes or trees and recall the lighting of the nearby Tivoli Gardens.

Jacobsen designed the interiors of the Royal Hotel as a series of naturalistic vignettes. In this series of pastels from 1956, he established the palette of green hues and wood paneling, the layering of vistas, and the subtle lighting schemes that would unite the hotel's different spaces.

→
Sketch of the winter garden.
↘
Sketch of the dining room.
↘ ↘
Sketch of the vestibule.

↓
Perspective drawing of the winter garden.
This drawing from 1958 depicts the winter garden as a transparent volume that connects the lower floors of the hotel.

VINTERHAVEN SET FRA HOTELLOBBY

←

Exterior of the SAS House. Forty-one years after the building's completion, the exterior of the SAS House preserves Jacobsen's original distinction between base and tower and the rectilinear grid of the curtain wall still impresses with its atmospheric effects and irregular reflections. Around the lobby area, however, most of the shops have been removed and the signage discarded.

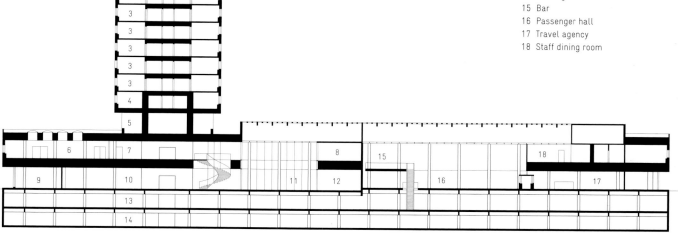

←

Longitudinal section, SAS House, 1:600.
The courtyards of the early schemes were
transformed into a top-lit restaurant, a
winter garden, and the air terminal atrium.
A pair of basements below street level
contained a parking garage and a wide
range of storage and maintenance facilities.

1 Mechanical equipment and sauna
2 Suites
3 Typical guest rooms
4 Staff services
5 Administration
6 Restaurant
7 Vestibule
8 Bar
9 Shops
10 Hotel lobby
11 Winter garden
12 Snack bar seating area
13 Service basement
14 Parking basement
15 Bar
16 Passenger hall
17 Travel agency
18 Staff dining room

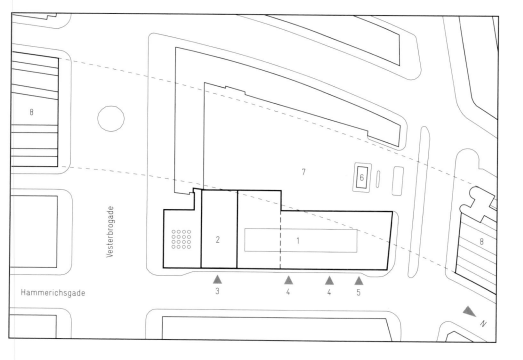

←

Site plan, SAS House, 1:2000.

1 Two-story building with Royal Hotel
   and SAS air terminal
2 Twenty-story tower
3 Entrance to hotel lobby
4 Entrances to passenger hall
5 Entrance to travel agency
6 Service station
7 Parking and bus stand
8 Railroad trench

First-floor plan, SAS House, 1:600.

1 Pastry shop
2 Perfume shop
3 Fur shop
4 Silver and porcelain shop
5 Newsstand
6 Flower shop
7 Photography shop
8 Jewelry shop
9 Tobacco shop
10 Chocolate shop
11 Entrance to hotel
12 Hotel lobby
13 Reception
14 Elevators
15 Stair
16 Public telephones
17 Winter garden
18 Ramp to parking
19 Loading dock
20 Snack bar kitchens
21 Snack bar seating area
22 Entrances to air terminal
23 Passenger hall
24 Exit to buses
25 Entry from buses
26 Stair to bar and basement
27 Public telephones
28 Luggage rooms
29 Bank
30 Offices
31 Travel agency
32 Car rental

Second-floor plan, SAS House, 1:600.

1 Elevators
2 Vestibule
3 Main dining room
4 Private dining rooms
5 Sitting rooms
6 Opening to winter garden
7 Bar
8 Cloakroom
9 Scullery
10 Service corridor
11 Hot kitchen
12 Cold kitchen
13 Smørrebrød kitchen
14 Pastry kitchen
15 Room service
16 Restrooms
17 Bar
18 Open to passenger hall
19 Staff dining room
20 Staff kitchen
21 Airline offices
22 Conference room
23 Staff stair

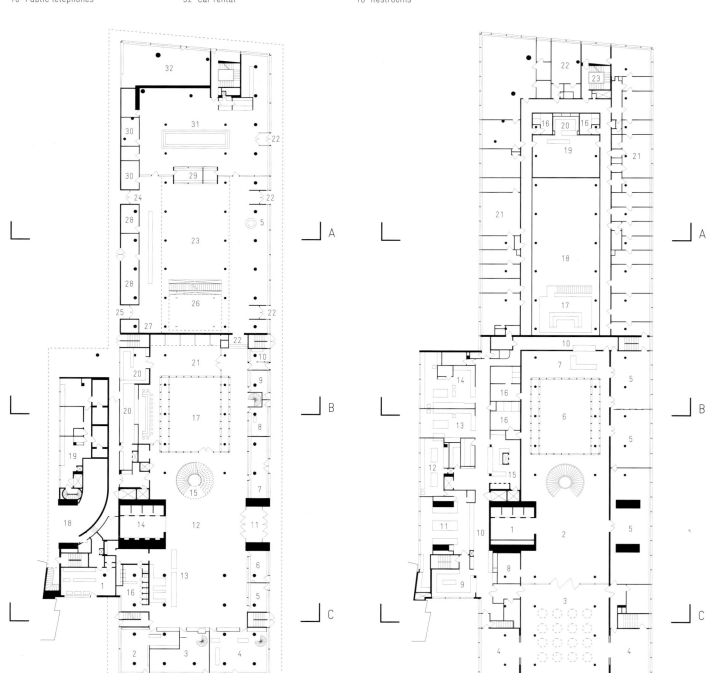

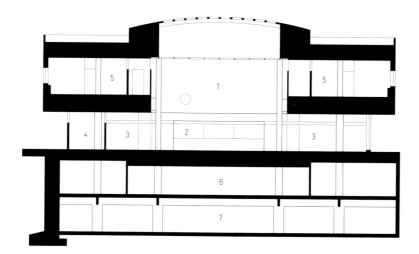

←

Cross section through the passenger hall
of the air terminal, 1:300.

1 Passenger hall
2 Bank
3 Aisles to travel agency
4 Luggage room
5 Airline offices
6 Rest area for passengers
7 Parking basement

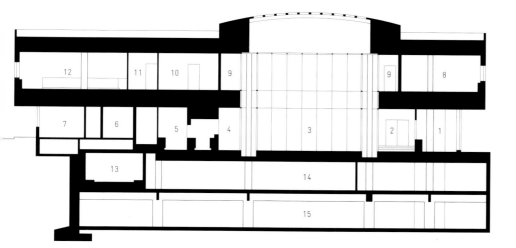

←

Cross section through the winter garden of
the Royal Hotel, 1:300.

 1 Jewelry shop
 2 Entrance to air terminal
 3 Winter garden
 4 Snack bar
 5 Snack bar kitchen
 6 Storage
 7 Loading dock
 8 Sitting room
 9 Passages to the bar
10 Restrooms
11 Service corridor
12 Smørrebrød kitchen
13 Ramp to parking
14 Service basement
15 Parking basement

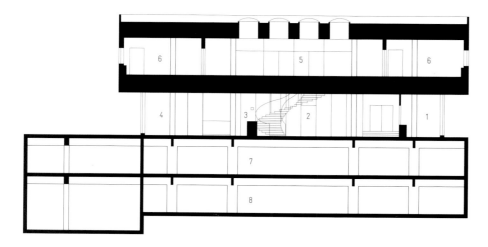

←

Cross section through the lobby and
restaurant of the Royal Hotel, 1:300.

1 Newsstand
2 Lobby
3 Reception
4 Public telephones
5 Main dining room
6 Private dining rooms
7 Service basement
8 Parking basement

↑
Detail of the air terminal travel agency.
Panels of quartersawn wenge combined
modular construction and natural pattern
into taut surfaces of suspended texture.

↙ ↓
Woven wool carpets designed for the
Royal Hotel. Jacobsen used geometry and
a palette of muted colors to create abstract equivalents to the subtle patterns
of wood and stone.

↓
Woven wool carpets designed for the
guest rooms. The rooms were carpeted
in different colorways of a single design:
a field of irregular dots on a neutral
background that changed appearance
according to the light.

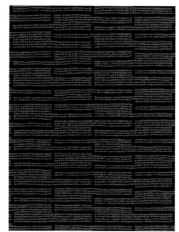
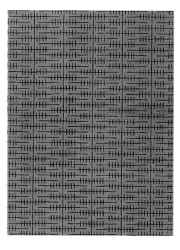

celebration of nature was an end in itself, allowing Jacobsen to master pattern and heralding the abstract surfaces to come. Even in the isolated prisms and gridded surfaces that characterized the later work, we find interior plantings and patterned surfaces of wood, glass, and stone that reiterate Jacobsen's devotion to the textures and variation of the plant world. While he was by no means unique in his use of nature as a creative wellspring, the combination of his veneration of the plant world and a willingness to use contemporary technology produced buildings that appear utterly contemporary forty years after their construction.

↓
Project for a single-family house, late 1940s. This watercolor of a simple brick house distilled Jacobsen's integrated conception of house and garden into a single iconic image. The large window overlooking the garden is filled with hanging flowers. While the patio extends the floor of the dwelling into the site, the grid of pavers is eroded by clusters of flowers and tall grasses. Along the edge of the site, a hedge obscures the immediate surroundings and creates a cultivated equivalent to the distant line of the sea.

Jacobsen's efforts at integrating architecture and landscape began in the late 1920s with the single-family houses that were the basis of his early practice. After graduating from the Royal Academy in 1926, he had a brief apprenticeship in the office of Poul Holsøe, the city architect of Copenhagen, but soon established his own office, in 1927. Around this time, vast areas of undeveloped land were being opened to private development as the Strandvejen highway was built along the coast north of Copenhagen. It was in the new garden suburbs along the highway that Jacobsen would spend the first decade of his career, constructing variations on the traditional Danish brick house. Between 1927 and 1933 alone he designed nearly forty houses, most of them in the Charlottenlund district, since renamed Ordrup. In many instances along Gotfred Rodes Vej, Hegelsvej, and other newly platted streets, Jacobsen's small villas ran contiguous or were separated by a single lot. While the houses continued the traditional Danish formula of a two-story brick box with a tiled roof, Jacobsen removed any hint of ornament and rearranged the windows to increase natural light and views of the surrounding landscape. As he reduced the traditional house to its essential form, Jacobsen added projecting wings, arbors, and terraces that extended the living space into the site, and by the early 1930s, he was designing the house and the garden as a unified composition. In the town halls that followed in Aarhus and Søllerød, the buildings were designed as staggered volumes that blended into the surrounding parkland. Meticulously designed paving and planting schemes completed the effect of civic gardens.

Like most Danish Jews, Jacobsen fled to Sweden in late 1943 to avoid deportation to the Nazi concentration camps. The last of his buildings to be completed before he and his wife became refugees would herald the next phase of Jacobsen's formal development. The factory for Sjællands Oddes Fiskerøgeri A/S, also known as the Fish Smokehouse, is set on a plateau overlooking the North Sea ninety kilometers from Copenhagen. Low buildings for handling fish and extracting roe were constructed along a long brick wall that culminates in a trio of massive chimneys that serve the smoking facility. A small monument in whitewashed brick, the smokehouse surpassed Jacobsen's previous attempts at integrating a building into its site. By dispensing with landscape treatments and designing the building as a bulwark against wind and rain, he fused location, climate, and program into a single elemental form.

Following his return from Sweden, Jacobsen's work underwent a profound transformation. The integration of the constructed and natural worlds remained the basis of his artistic vision, but the products of that vision became increasingly abstract in form and industrial in technique. As his buildings shifted toward asymmetrical compositions of unadorned planes, their interaction with their surroundings became increasingly direct. While Jacobsen continued to design gardens for his buildings, those gardens took the form of planted courtyards or stepped terraces that reconstructed the site.

The first evidence of this interweaving of terrain and building can be seen in Jacobsen's Søholm row house development

↑
Sjællands Odde Fish Smokehouse, Odden
Harbor, 1943. At this dramatic site overlooking the North Sea, Jacobsen created
a miniature monument that was both
a crown and the culmination of the cliff.

↖
Helge Wandel House, Gentofte, 1934–35.
As Jacobsen designed variations on
the traditional Danish brick house, he
extended the dwelling into the site with
extensions, arbors, and paved surfaces.

←
Hasselbalch House, Charlottenlund,
1934–36. Pools and the winter garden in
the background allowed the family contact
with nature, regardless of the season. At
the corner of the house, a *blomstervindue*
(flower window) allowed light to penetrate
deep into the living room.

↙
Brobjerg House, Charlottenlund, 1932–33.
While plant-filled windows blurred the
boundaries to the natural world outside,
the water garden beyond allowed the
house to dissolve into the lawn.

completed in 1950 in Klampenborg, a hundred meters down the Strandvejen from the Bellavista apartments. Around 1946, a group of investors purchased the Søholm estate, the site of a recently demolished nineteenth-century villa, and commissioned Jacobsen to design a series of multifamily residences. The property was developed in phases; a 1948 site plan depicts two rows of two-story terraced houses and a band of three-story houses at the back of the site. Once the first row of houses was completed in 1950, Jacobsen moved his family into the southernmost unit. A projecting bay accommodated his study on the upper floor, while a meeting room for his office was located in the half-basement below.

By fracturing the traditional row of houses into a chain of offset blocks, Jacobsen was able to provide natural light to every room and to create greater privacy for the front entry and the rear garden of each unit. Each of the units occupied a deep lot with a uniform width of 8.75 meters. At the north end of the lots, house and patio were treated as an interlocking composition enclosed by low granite walls that extended to the edge of the property. Jacobsen terraced the site to elevate the houses above the driveway. From the sidewalk, a path and steps lead up to the entries, while ramped driveways provide access to the sunken garages. Loan restrictions limited the houses to 110 square meters, so Jacobsen used a variety of overlapping spaces to ensure a feeling of spaciousness. On the ground floor, a double-height dining room faces onto a terrace and contains the stair to the living room that occupies the top floor. Beyond the stair, three bedrooms look out onto side and rear gardens. The living room provides an expansive view of the sea and culminates in a small balcony overlooking the rear garden.

The diagonal layout of the Søholm terrace houses was the culmination of the experiment that had begun in 1935 at the Bellavista apartments. After Bellavista and his competition-winning scheme, with Erik Møller, for Aarhus Town Hall, Jacobsen's focus shifted from single-family houses to large-scale residential developments and public buildings. As his residential work grew in scale Jacobsen developed the staggered site plan as a way to break long rows of housing, to introduce an intermediate scale, and to counter the potentially overwhelming effect of repetitive units.

The second phase of the Søholm complex was completed in 1952 with the construction of the three-story row at the back of the property. The final phase was completed in 1954. Rather than constructing another row of terraced houses as originally planned, Jacobsen designed a group of one-story houses set back from the busy coastal highway, in this way preserving the views of the three-story houses at the back of the property. This adjustment of the original scheme illustrates both Jacobsen's pragmatic approach and his flexibility in creating compositions of multiple buildings.

In 1951 Jacobsen was chosen to design an elementary school in Gentofte Kommune, outside of Copenhagen. Completed six years later, the Munkegård School was a landmark of Jacobsen's career, combining his fascination with landscape design and the modular building forms that characterized his work after 1948.

View from the coastal highway, Søholm row house development, Klampenborg, 1946–54. The gray yellow bricks, the rough granite wall, and the dense vegetation that obscures the interior of the site from the highway blend into a unified composition of house and garden.

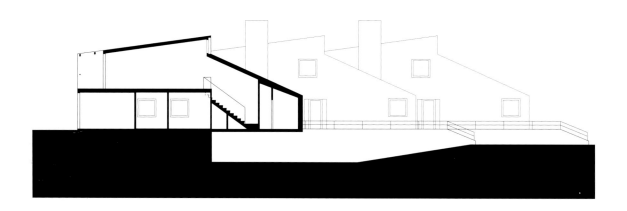

Phase Two

N

Phase Three

Phase One

Strandvejen

↖

Section, Søholm houses, phase one 1946–50, 1:250. Jacobsen terraced the site to create basement parking, individual entrances, and private gardens at the rear of each house. Inside, he located the bedrooms on the first floor, providing the living room at the top of the stairs with panoramic views of the Øresund.

←

Site plan, Søholm, 1:1200. The original plan for the property combined parallel bands of two-story row houses with three-story houses along the back of the site. Following the construction of the three-story houses in 1951 (phase two), Jacobsen altered the original scheme and designed a set of one-story houses that preserved the eastward views. The result is a small neighborhood with three different house types that are united by a sensitivity to placement and craftsmanship.

↗→→

Views of Søholm houses, phase one. In the front, raised entries alternated with recessed driveways leading to the garages below. Each house opened onto a back garden, where walls of woven willow and the houses' staggered arrangement provided a sense of privacy. Next to the coastal highway, Strandvejen, Jacobsen's own garden was protected from the wind and traffic noise by stands of bamboo.

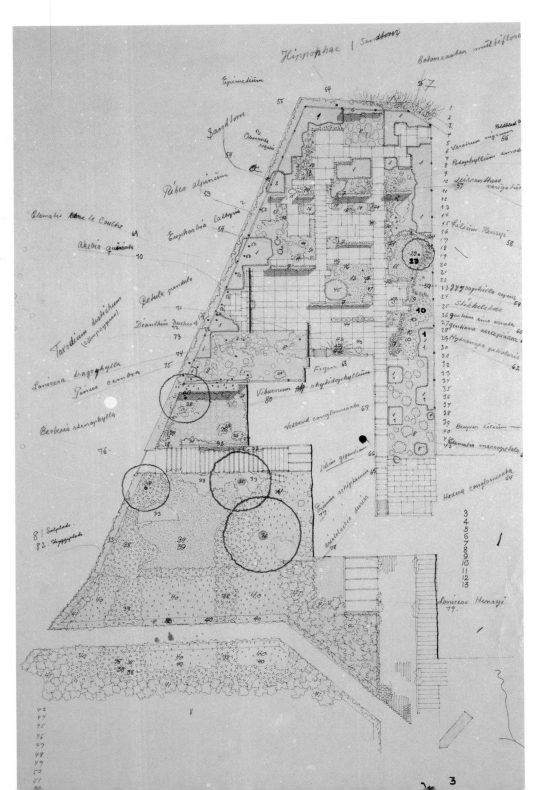

View of Jacobsen's garden from the second-floor balcony, Søholm. Jacobsen chose the house with the largest garden, located next to Strandvejen, for himself and his family. The garden was paved with slabs of Porsgruun marble and organized around parallel walls of larch that were clipped to create thin screens of varying heights. In spite of the detailed planting scheme he created initially, Jacobsen continued to rearrange the plants and introduce new species for the rest of his life.

Planting scheme of Jacobsen's garden. An avid gardener, Jacobsen used the 300 square meters as a testing ground for juxtapositions of color and texture that would inform his architecture and textile designs. Jacobsen's own partially annotated plan displays both horticultural expertise and the care with which he arranged the species. The accompanying key was published with a later redrawn version of the plan.

Planting Key

1 Umbrella bamboo	20 David viburnum	41 Chromeflower barberry	62 May apple
2 Fountain bamboo	21 Fingerleaf flower	42 Amaryllis	63 Downy clematis
3 Dwarf bamboo	22 Bayberry	43 Yellow tree peony	64 English ivy
4 Arrowhead bamboo	23 Princess tree	44 Lily of the Nile	65 Schipka laurel
5 Palm-Leaf bamboo	24 Staghorn sumac	45 Sea buckthorn	66 Sunset lily
6 Common yew	25 Japanese maple	46 Foxtail lily	67 English ivy
7 Japanese larch	26 Bird's-nest spruce	47 White ash	68 Weeping fig
8 Various herbs	27 Sulphur heart ivy	48 Adam's needle tree	69 White clematis
9 Fingerleaf flower	28 Hazelwort	49 Japanese pieris	70 Chocolate vine
10 Sargent hydrangea	29 Warty barberry	50 Winter heather	71 White birch
11 Pachysandra	30 Staghorn sumac	51 Giant reed	72 Red dianthus
12 Creeping euonymus	31 Cutleaf stephanandra	52 Scotch pine	73 Bald cyprus
13 Chilean wine palm	32 Dawn redwood	53 Alpine gooseberry	74 Chinese honeysuckle
14 Various orchids	33 Cutleaf stephanandra	54 Caper spurge	75 Arolla pine
15 Birdcage	34 Evergreen cotoneaster	55 Silver grass	76 Yellow barberry
16 Zebra grass	35 Black locust	56 Black false hellebore	77 Schipka laurel
17 Maiden grass	36 Elm	57 Multicolored cotoneaster	78 Dutchman's-pipe
18 Blue oat grass	37 Golden chain tree	58 Turk's cap lily	79 Evergreen honeysuckle
19 Tree peony	38 Scarlet firethorn	59 Creeping baby's breath	80 Leatherleaf viburnum
	39 Bearberry cotoneaster	60 Willow gentian	81 Sun terrace
	40 English ivy	61 Autumn gentian	82 Shade terrace

→

First-floor plan, Munkegård School, Gentofte, 1948–57, 1:500. A series of parallel corridors provided access to pairs of standard classrooms, and to a two-story building at the back of the site containing special classrooms. The gymnasium building, a kindergarten, and a bicycle storage framed an entry courtyard that served as a playground.

↑

Watercolor perspective of the Munkegård School. Jacobsen's lush aerial view of the complex from 1948 illustrates his original scheme for the school complex. As the number of classrooms grew, the grid was extended west toward the playing field, and the gymnasia on the lower right were rotated parallel to the corridors and auditorium.

1 Standard classrooms
2 Coatrooms
3 Courtyards
4 Corridor
5 Metalworking shop
6 Woodworking shop
7 Library
8 Needlework shop
9 Faculty lounge
10 Auditorium
11 Stage
12 Administration
13 Gymnasiums
14 Locker rooms
15 Boys' toilets
16 Girls' toilets
17 Bicycle storage
18 Entry gate
19 Kindergarten

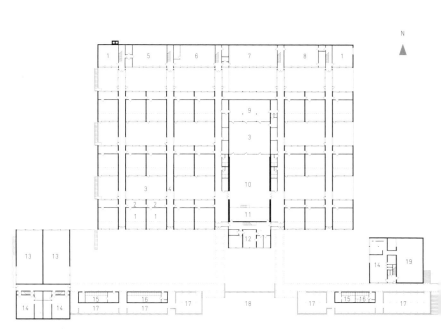

The building was designed for 850 children, and Jacobsen treated it as a series of smaller spaces that expanded from the classroom to the shared corridors to the whole building. In a very literal way, the spatial organization of the school reflected the process of socialization that characterizes the experience of childhood. The result was a well-lit village of intimate proportions and tactile richness, carefully tailored to the physical scale of the children.

The key innovation of the Munkegård School was that its classrooms were arranged in pairs in a grid to provide each group of children with an enclosed courtyard for play and outdoor lessons. Between the classrooms, intimate corridors, each painted a different color, were punctuated by broad windows looking onto the adjacent courtyards. Jacobsen treated the courtyards as individual gardens, each with a unique paving pattern, plating scheme, and a sculpture or casting he selected himself. While the classrooms were the product of prolonged research into the requirements of the students and the optimum distribution of sunlight, the courtyards are the real substance of the building. In concert with the parallel corridors and the modules of paired classrooms, they form a matrix of light and nature that resembles a plan for a utopian community.

Confronted with a sloping site, Jacobsen created a plateau for the school building and located the gymnasiums and playing fields on the low ground at the west end of the property. At the edge of the plateau, the grid is sheared to reveal the serrated profile of the classrooms and corridors.

As he refined the design for the Munkegård School, Jacobsen began work on a housing scheme for the municipal government of Søllerød, where he had completed the town hall in 1942. Although the plan was not realized, it demonstrates the degree to which the atrium had entered Jacobsen's formal vocabulary as a device for combining the site and the building. The Carlsminde development was designed for a sloping site that faced south toward a park with a small lake. Forty-two courtyard houses were arranged in rows of seven or eight units that ran perpendicular to the slope. At the top of the property, Jacobsen designed a trio of two-story buildings to preserve an open space with old trees as a playground. Behind each row, along the north side of the houses, a driveway provided access to the garages at the edge of the site. Within the houses, rooms were terraced to follow the slope of the hillside, allowing daylight to reach the interior courtyards and the south-facing bedrooms above them. The lowest rooms were the living rooms that spanned the width of the houses and opened onto a string of paved terraces with views of the lake. The section through a typical house reveals Jacobsen's combination of terrace and courtyard as a means of providing spatial variety and natural light to the one-story buildings. As at Søholm, the houses are handled as extensions of the site, providing intimate contact with the topography within the repetitive framework of the buildings. At the same time, the courtyard provided Jacobsen with an instrument for incorporating episodes of natural experience within his buildings, regardless of location or terrain.

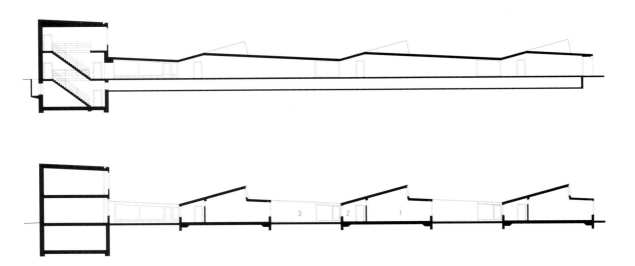

↑
Section through a corridor (top) and classrooms (bottom), Munkegård School, 1:500.
The large classroom windows captured the
sunlight and spread it throughout the
school. Glass transoms between classroom and vestibule allowed the light to
continue to the back of each small building. The long straight corridors were covered with undulating ceilings that
provided spatial variety and prevented an
institutional effect.

1   Standard classroom
2   Coatroom
3   Courtyard

↓
Aerial view of the Munkegård School.
The south-facing school was constructed
of parallel yellow brick walls with roofs of
galvanized aluminum. Clerestory windows
allowed the low winter sun to reach deep
into each classroom. The back of the two-
story building was covered in a wall of
cement board panels and wood windows
that served as a prototype for Jacobsen's
glass buildings of the mid-1950s.

View of a Munkegård School courtyard.
At the west end of the building, the single
courtyards had cantilevered concrete
stairs leading down to the playing field.
↓
View from the playing fields of the classrooms and gymnasium. This view reveals
the school as a built-up plateau overlooking an open playing area. The two-story
volume of the auditorium at the back
protrudes above the grid of classrooms.

←

A typical courtyard of the Munkegård School. The courtyards provided space for play and outdoor lessons. Each one was given an individual character through a unique scheme of paving and plantings. In addition, Jacobsen selected a sculpture or a casting of an ancient relic to provide the little gardens with a plastic focal point.

↙

A typical classroom of the Munkegård School. Natural light and ventilation were the determining factors in the design of the classrooms. In 1955, a full-scale test classroom was constructed in a nearby field to determine the ceiling angle and window dimensions necessary for proper daylighting. The final design combined extensive windows and a special recessed light fixture to provide even illumination regardless of the season.

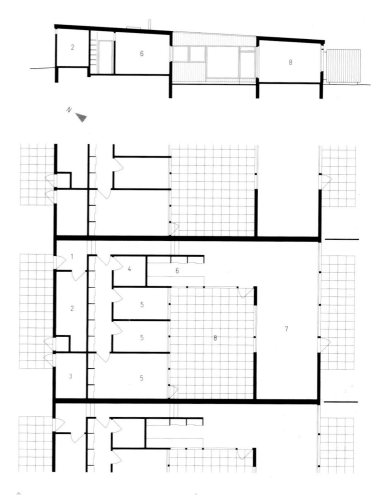

↑

Section and plan, Carlsminde row houses, 1955, 1:200. The houses took advantage of the sloping site by placing the bedrooms at the higher elevation, increasing their separation from the living room across the courtyard.

1 Vestibule
2 Storage
3 Bicycle storage
4 Bathroom
5 Bedrooms
6 Kitchen-dining area
7 Living room
8 Courtyard

↓

Detail of model, Carlsminde row houses. The courtyards featured color panels to heighten the effect of changing light. Both the courts and south walls of the living rooms were enclosed with wood windows and cement board panels.

Aerial view of St. Catherine's College, Oxford, 1959–64. This view locates the college on an open plain along a tributary of the Rover Cherwell, outside the old part of Oxford. Entry to the college is afforded via a small road around the round bicycle shed, past the master's house and over the canal that separates the bounded precinct of the college from the suburban landscape.

In contrast to the dense medieval clusters of the traditional Oxford colleges, Jacobsen developed St. Catherine's as a series of buildings arranged on a paved plinth with a variety of planted areas.
All of the buildings are constructed of pre-cast columns and beams.

Lecture room looking toward a residential building.

Courtyard looking toward the bell tower with a lecture building on the left.

Jacobsen's most literal creation of an artificial landscape was completed in 1964 on a paved plinth along the River Cherwell in Oxford, England. Four years earlier, Jacobsen had been commissioned by the dons of the newly chartered St. Catherine's College to build the first new residential college in Oxford in 400 years. The site was a flat parcel that had served as a dumping ground. Jacobsen constructed a raised platform on which to build the largest of the gardens that had preoccupied him since the 1930s.

Entered by a bridge across a watercourse that served as both boundary and garden, the college was composed of free-standing buildings that were arranged around a porous quadrangle. Between the buildings, a uniform grid of concrete pavers that continued the structural module of the buildings was eroded by irregular groups of plants. At either end of the quad, low walls of brick and trellises covered with vines framed views of a circular meadow and the enormous cyprus tree that was the centerpiece of the composition.

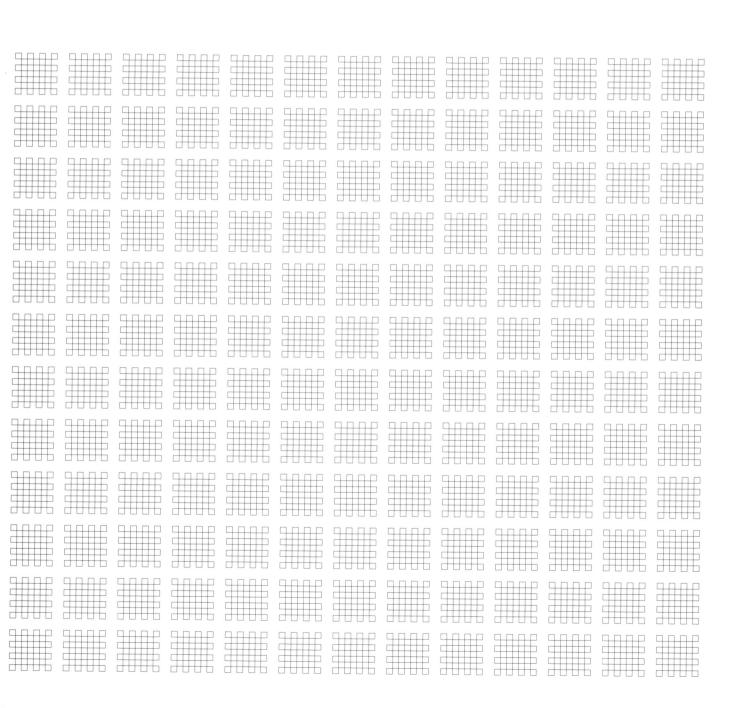

↑
Room 606, Royal Hotel, SAS House,
Copenhagen, 1955–60. The bedroom is
dominated by a band of windows that
connects each hotel room with the continuous web of glass and metal covering the
tower. During the long, overcast winters
that are typical in Denmark, the expanse of
glass captures the low sun and creates a
chamber of warm, pale green light.

Along the outer wall of Room 606, a continuous band of glass faces south over Vesterbrogade, filling the room with natural light. Aluminum mullions divide the glass into twelve windows, each 60 by 120 centimeters, that frame sweeping views of Tivoli Gardens and the Hovedbanegård, the central rail station. Within the shallow zone between the interior wood paneling and the outer face of the mullions, layers of glass and fabric evidence Jacobsen's attention to physical comfort and his preoccupation with overlapping views and ideal proportions. At every third window, a steel frame provides an inswing window for natural ventilation. Behind the dark blue valance, curtains and roller blinds of light green mesh and heavy drapes of Jacobsen's own design allow variable levels of light and privacy. At either end of the window wall, where the inner walls stop short of the glass, thin partitions, painted blue to match the plastic-laminate sill and sound-insulated, fill the gap between structure and skin. While the mullions establish a vertical rhythm that modulates the expanse of glass, the 1:2 module of the windows recalls Jacobsen's training at the Royal Academy, in the last days of neoclassicism. Throughout the SAS House, a variety of traditional architectural strategies, from axial symmetry to nineteenth-century set pieces, reflected Jacobsen's education at the cusp between classicism and modernism.

The windows that open the interior of 606 to the center of Copenhagen also mark its direct connection to the curtain wall that was Jacobsen's ultimate synthesis of geometric form and natural phenomena. The facades of the hotel tower are composed of a grid of aluminum members that frame alternating bands of clear and colored glass. The transparent units are insulated windows for the hotel rooms, while the opaque gray green panels conceal the low concrete walls that project above and below the floor slabs. This curtain wall was the product of Jacobsen's divergent activities in

Room 606. Mesh curtains filter the daylight and obscure the views into the rooms
while still allowing the guests to enjoy the
scenery. Outside, the open trench in front
of the central station extends beneath the
SAS site. This trench required the hotel
tower to be located close to Vesterbrogade, at the widest part of the property.

architecture and the applied arts. In the ten years leading up to the SAS House, Jacobsen had used both textiles and glass walls as a means of exploring pattern and color. Pattern making was central to Jacobsen's artistic activity. The landscape and botanical paintings of his youth had been formative training in recognizing subtle interactions of outlines and textures, and Jacobsen started to design textiles in the 1940s. His first designs were paintings of flowers and plants, but after World War II, as his architecture became influenced by the repetitive logic of industrial production, Jacobsen's textile designs became correspondingly abstract; scenes of nature were distilled into surfaces of solid color and shape. In the early 1950s, as he developed modular skins of glass and metal to cover his public buildings, he continued to design patterns for curtains and carpets.

For Jacobsen, these seemingly very different pursuits were united by a handful of aesthetic goals, including a reduced palette of forms and materials, the cultivation of rich surfaces, and the use of hanging objects to create an effect of weightlessness. At the SAS House, architecture and textile design converged—the fixed pattern of metal and the constantly shifting effects of color and transparency created a vitreous tapestry visible from the edge of the city. Today, the exterior of the building remains relatively intact and continues to provide lessons in the emotive power of abstract form and in the potential in the intersection of technology and the environment.

→
Watercolor of the SAS House with signage for the "Hotel Globe," 1957. This water-color study of the SAS House features a curtain wall on the long sides of the tower and end walls of black stone. Along Hammerichsgade, signage for the Hotel Globe marks the entry to what would become the Royal Hotel. After the hotel consultant hired by the airline pointed out the desirability of corner rooms with wraparound windows, Jacobsen was instructed to provide a continuous glass exterior.

The first public drawings of the SAS House were published in Copenhagen newspapers in 1956. The resemblance between Jacobsen's building and the Lever House in New York was immediately condemned by local critics who feared the importation of American corporate architecture and the transformation of Copenhagen's picturesque skyline of medieval towers and steeples. However, rather than an imitation of Gordon Bunshaft's design for Skidmore, Owings & Merrill or a generic building imported from abroad, Jacobsen's building would be a monumental intersection of abstract form and local light.

Rising twenty stories above the low buildings along Hammerichsgade, the tower of the SAS Royal Hotel was clad in delicate walls of glass designed to reflect the clouds. The mutable surface still reflects the skies over Copenhagen, changing in color and opacity from hour to hour. The elegant cladding of the building appears inevitable today, yet it was the result of an exhaustive study of texture and color. Jacobsen approached the design of the tower as an exercise in surface treatment, akin to one of his woven curtains. In fact, the number of exterior studies among the original SAS House drawings is exceeded only by the sketches for the hotel guest rooms. One of the first studies, in Jacobsen's own hand, depicts an alternating pattern of solid and transparent units that presages the curtains and light fixtures of the hotel interior. Even at this early stage, the shading indicates changes in reflection as the tower rises, while a deep shadow line between base and tower illustrates Jacobsen's desire for continuity with the neighboring building. The textile motif was taken further in a rough sketch of yellow bands of glass or metal, overlaid with expressed columns that emphasize the height of the tower. Jacobsen had already recessed the glass walls of the third floor, occupied by maintenance offices and equipment rooms, to provide a gap between tower and base.

Jacobsen's preferred method of design was perspective drawing, a product of his early experience as a watercolorist. Before embarking on a career in architecture, he had intended to be a painter, but Jacobsen's father had disapproved of the plan and steered his son toward the School of Architecture at the Royal Academy. Throughout his career, Jacobsen used watercolors as a decisive tool in winning architectural competitions, placing his increasingly abstract forms in lush aerial-view illustrations filled with foliage, people, and cobalt blue skies.

A set of perspective studies from late 1955, drawn from the vantage point of Tivoli Gardens, records Jacobsen's search for the proper surface treatment of the hotel tower. The watercolor of the "Hotel Globe," as it was then called, depicts the sidewalls of the tower clad in green glass and capped with end walls of stone. The contrast between perpendicular surfaces of glass and of stone was one of Jacobsen's preferred formal strategies; he had employed it in all of his previous curtain wall projects. The use of contrasting materials in this case probably also reflected his concerns about the bulk of the tower. The SAS House was much larger than any of Jacobsen's previous buildings, and the use of two distinct surfaces emphasized the tower as a set of planes,

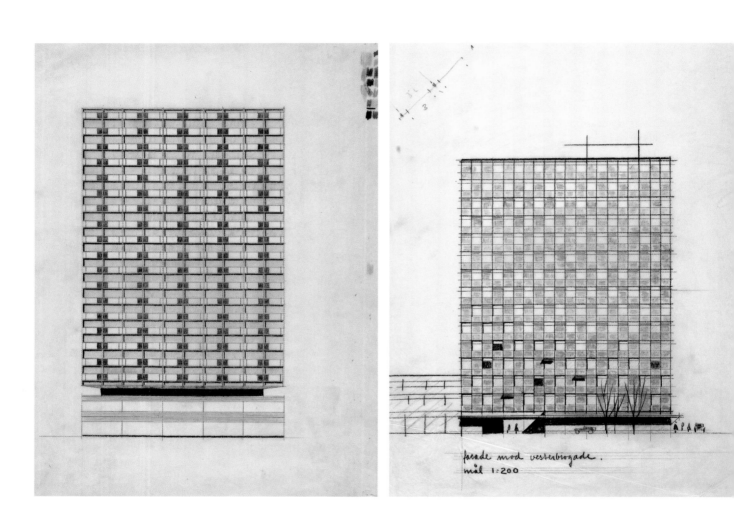

facade mod vesterbrogade.
mål 1:200

↖ ↑

Facade studies, SAS House, 1956.
Jacobsen's early sketches for the tower
walls resemble his curtain fabric designs
from the same period. In an attempt to
give the large volume of the building an
animated surface that would register
shifts in light, he explored alternating
patterns of color and transparent glass,
colored metal panels, and shallow
assemblies of metal and stone.

rather than a single volume. Fortunately for the guests, this scheme was not realized. Alberto Kappenberger, the hotel manager hired by SAS, recognized the economic value of corner rooms with two exposures and bathrooms with views of the town hall; the airline would ultimately insist on windows for the end walls. Later drawings of the tower depict a variety of window treatments and materials, including square panels with punched openings and horizontal bands of glass and metal. Of course, all of the guest rooms would have operable windows, and it is likely this fact that pushed Jacobsen toward a continuous glass skin.

Even after Jacobsen had decided on alternating bands of transparent and colored glass, he struggled with the final color scheme. By the early 1950s, Jacobsen had evolved his own vocabulary of color, which was dominated by subtle shades of gray, green, and blue; as his work became increasingly geometric, his palette returned to the colors of the plant world. Working to define the character of his largest building to date, Jacobsen experienced some doubt. (The bright colors of the early facade sketches reappeared in a drawing of a yellow tower and blue podium that emphasized the division between object and base.)

The final design for the exterior used a pair of contrasting materials that, while similar in color, reacted to sunlight in dramatically different ways. Above the recessed, glass-faced storefronts below, the upper level containing the airline offices and the hotel's public areas was covered by a grid of steel plates coated with matte gray green enamel that absorbed light and strengthened the impression of a heavy base. For the tower, the color of the opaque glass was the key to Jacobsen's goal of a continuous surface. This gray-green shade was close enough to the matte enamel to relate the tower to the base but light enough to blend in with the reflections on the clear windows. The overall effect was of a single surface of glass that shifted in color and density according to the angle of the sun and the thickness of the clouds. At the top of the tower, stacked bands of opaque glass, similar to the capital on a classical column, crowned the building with a corona of reflected light.

Jacobsen's first curtain wall, completed in 1953 on a modest eight-story office building a few blocks from Hammerichsgade, had been constructed of a heavy timber frame covered with sheet metal. The much larger scale of the SAS House allowed him to employ the most advanced technology available. Working with the engineers at Josef Gartner Inc., a curtain wall specialist in Dortmund, Germany, Jacobsen developed a system of extruded aluminum mullions that were bolted to the low concrete walls and infilled with horizontal muntins and steel frames for the operable windows. Frames for operable windows are wider than the channels supporting fixed glass panes, but by using inswing windows, Jacobsen was able to set the frames behind the aluminum grid and thus maintain a consistent appearance on the exterior surface. In addition, open inswing windows would appear as voids in the aluminum grid rather than projections that would break the surface and reflect light at different angles.

↖ ↑

Perspective drawings, SAS House, 1957. After the dimensions of the building were finalized, the tower cladding was developed in a series of drawings from the perspective of Tivoli Gardens. A scheme of precast concrete panels with square windows resembled Jacobsen's own Stelling House of 1937, located a kilometer away on Gammeltorv. The final scheme of an all-glass wall used narrow panels of glass and closely spaced mullions to emphasize the vertical thrust of the tower.

→

Color study, SAS House, c.1957. The horizontal division of base and tower was emphasized by recessing the third floor, producing a dark line of shade at the junction between the two forms. Jacobsen considered using contrasting colors to further the independence of the parts. The eventual solution used contrasting shades of a single color and different surface textures to create a more unified composition.

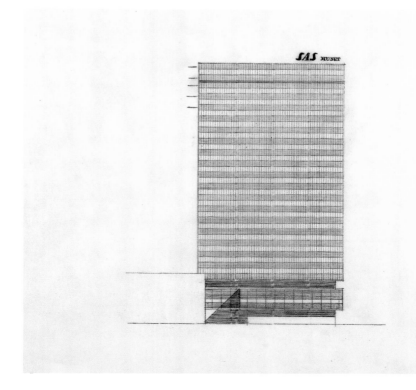

Jacobsen manipulated the curtain wall's aluminum framework to emphasize the height of the tower. The mullions, tapered to eighteen millimeters on their outer face, project beyond the horizontal muntins to reflect light in unbroken vertical rays. The appearance of the corners was also critical to the intended effect of weightlessness. To achieve this, Jacobsen designed the vertical edges of the tower as recessed voids. A special L-shaped extrusion created continuous pockets of shadow that split the prism into pairs of hovering planes. Viewed from the street, the corner windows and their chamfered mullions make the floor trays appear to float.

In a published statement that omitted any mention of the difficult work that had preoccupied him for much of 1956, Jacobsen described the result as a set of simple facts:

On artistic grounds it was important to try and make as light a building as possible, because of the great height and mass of the block which would easily overpower the surrounding buildings and appear to give an unfortunate heaviness over the neighboring Tivoli Gardens.

One grey-green sheet of glass divided up by anodized aluminum mullions in a unity without special architectonic divisions was the only solution which I thought would give the least dominating sort of building. The glass colour was selected with reference to the sky and the reflection of the clouds. A stronger coloured glass would probably, under some conditions of light, seem gayer and more lively, but in other light the effect would have been too strong and bombastic.

The reflection of the weather gives the building a changing character which, I felt, was more important than striving for a stronger effect. The light, high block needs a heavier base, which is why a darker, grey-green enamel cladding was chosen.

(International Lighting Review 12, no. 2 [1961], p. 42)

In a perfunctory assessment published in *Zodiac* in 1961, Henry-Russell Hitchcock, one of the early impresarios of modern architecture, began a brief review of the building's exterior by faulting its location in the city center: "Although there is much nineteenth-century precedent for building a major hotel [downtown] . . . the air-terminal facilities are quite incidental—near a principal railway station, it seems curiously retardaire in an age of air and motor travel to choose such a location." Following a negative description of the surrounding area—"cluttered with neon signs"— Hitchcock addressed the tower. Leaving aside the questions of whether he visited the interior of the building or the season of his visit, his critique precisely identifies the qualities of scale and color that characterize Jacobsen's extraordinary skin:

But the tower itself is a disappointment. Although Jacobsen was no late convert to curtain-walling, having used it from the mid-50's on lower commercial structures, he seems to have exaggerated here the daintiness of scale in relation to total mass which is one of the

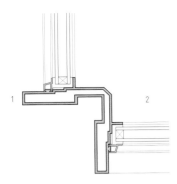
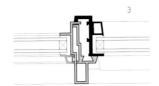
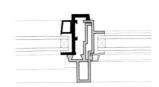
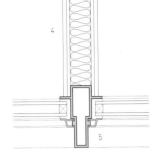

↑
Plan detail of curtain wall, SAS House, 1:5. The tower of the Royal Hotel was covered in a frame of aluminum extrusions that held panels of transparent and reflective glass. Operable window frames were set behind the aluminum structure to preserve the slender lines of the mullions.

1 Aluminum corner mullion
2 Fixed window
3 Operable window with steel frame
4 Insulated partition to concrete wall
5 Typical aluminum mullion

↓
Detail of the curtain wall. The aluminum mullions were spaced at sixty-centimeter intervals with alternating bands of 120-centimeter transparent and 168-centimeter opaque glass panels.

→
Wall section, 1:20. The low concrete parapets were covered in sheets of opaque glass. The windowsill was aligned with the top of the wood paneling, and an open metal grill below concealed heating and cooling equipment.

1 Reinforced concrete floor and parapet
2 Painted wood valance
3 Woven wool curtain
4 Nylon mesh curtain
5 Painted wallcovering
6 Plastic laminate on insulated partition
7 Aluminum air grill
8 Wenge paneling
9 Painted wood baseboard
10 Insulated window
11 Opaque glass pandrel

→→
View of the SAS House from across Vesterbrogade.

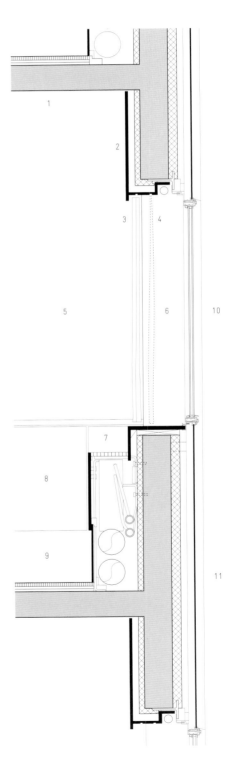

curtain-wall's chief visual disadvantages. The miniscule size, relatively and even absolutely speaking, of the panel units whether glazed or solid, the interior scale dimensions of the continuous mullions, above all the surprising proportion of solid to glazed panels—approximately 2 to 1 where in most curtain walls the proportion is nearer 1 to 2 or even more—have produced a surface that is excessively fragile without even suggesting transparency. The universal dark grey coloring, moreover, varied only by the letters SAS, placed like a monogram at the head of a sheet of letterpaper, is peculiarly unsuited to the grey skies of Copenhagen, however refreshing it might be in the summer climate of Milan.

The delicacy of the aluminum frame and the proportion of the opaque glass panels that Hitchcock faulted are, in fact, what account for the airy appearance of the tower. While designers of conventional curtain walls had pursued an effect of weightlessness through simple transparency, they had generally overlooked the darkness created by reflections. Jacobsen's sensitivity to light, honed through years of textile design and his earlier curtain walls, allowed him to create a glass surface that shifts back and forth from reflection to transmission, from surface to depth.

Views of the SAS House. The building dominated the skyline of central Copenhagen. Depending on weather and vantage point, the seventy-meter tower appeared as a series of transparent planes or as a solid prism that floated above the treetops.

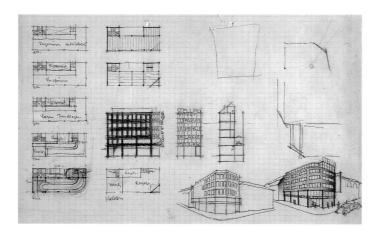

↑

Sketches of the Stelling House, c. 1934. A
series of small-scale pencil drawings depict the development of the Stelling House
in plan, elevation, and perspective. The division between a base of display windows
and a volume with punched openings was
present from the beginning. The three-
dimensional studies illustrate alternative
methods of turning the corner.

↙ ↓

Stelling House, Copenhagen, 1934–37.
Jacobsen's first building in the center of
the city provided the model for the gridded
surfaces of the SAS House and inspired the
division between a transparent base and
an opaque volume. This mixed-use building combined a two-story shop for an art
supply company with rented offices on the
upper floors.

Jacobsen's buildings became increasingly abstract after his return to Denmark in 1945. He began to abandon traditional Danish building techniques, in favor of new, lightweight methods of construction. This shift, from solid volumes of brick with punched window openings, in which surface and structure are integral, to modular frames covered with lightweight skins, occurred in a series of decisive steps. In the late 1940s, Jacobsen pulled apart the brick boxes of his prewar houses into parallel sets of load-bearing walls spanned by panels of glass and wood. These prototypical curtain walls were most apparent at Søholm and at the Munkegård School, and in the following decade they would be developed further in a series of private houses. As large-scale commissions returned to his office, Jacobsen's use of glass expanded from infill to envelope in a set of prismatic volumes that floated in the landscape. The SAS House would gather elements of these buildings into a single work, but he had in fact discovered the basic equation of glazed base and iridescent tower that would define the SAS House long before he adopted industrialized building techniques.

In 1934, Jacobsen was commissioned to design the Stelling House, a small commercial building located on a corner of Gammeltorv, an old square in the center of Copenhagen. The building combined a two-story shop for A. Stelling Farvehandel, the reputed art supply company, with three floors of rental offices and a penthouse apartment. Jacobsen's handling of the exterior reflected both the layered set of functions and a sensitivity to the historic area. While the rounded corner of the building and its alignment with the neighboring structures emphasized continuity with its surroundings, Jacobsen treated the retail store as a large-scale vitrine. To cover the upper portion of the building, which continued the cornice line of the adjacent structure, Jacobsen selected large Siegersdorfer tiles, glazed in a gray green tint that shifted color with the changing light.

The Stelling House was critical for Jacobsen in several respects. Even as the square windows and rounded corner displayed the continuing influence of the pioneering Swedish architect Erik Gunnar Asplund, Jacobsen's use of glazed tiles for cladding was a first step toward his curtain walls of the 1950s. In designing the building as a pair of stacked objects, Jacobsen created a model for the recessed ground floor of the SAS House and, more distantly, the pairing of base and tower along Hammerichsgade. The juxtaposition of transparent screens and solid walls was used in the early curtain wall buildings that lead up to the SAS House. As the emphasis in Jacobsen's work shifted from patterned structure to patterned surface, brick was replaced by stone tiles that were polished to a reflective gloss and used as the opaque equivalent of glass.

The first design where Jacobsen treated stone and glass as equivalent surfaces was an eight-story office building completed in 1953 for the construction company A. Jespersen and Sons. The Jespersen House featured Jacobsen's first curtain wall and served as the structural model for the tower of the Royal Hotel. The property was subject to an easement that guaranteed the occupants of a neighboring apartment building access to a parking area in the

A series of private houses in the mid-1950s adapted the wood curtain walls designed for the Munkegård School to domestic settings. Both of these houses, typical of Jacobsen's residential buildings from the 1950s, used brick bases and laminated timber beams to support light-weight pavilions of glass and wood. The wood-framed window walls allowed Jacobsen to experiment with proportions and pattern on a small scale.

↙
Siesby House, Virum, 1956–57.
↓
Kokfelt House, Tisvilde, 1955–56.

center of the block. Jacobsen placed the service core at the edge of the property and elevated the central office block on two enormous piers to create a porte cochere at street level. Inside, the piers were divided into paired columns that framed a central corridor on each of the seven floors. The property rights for the absent ground floor were transferred to the roof, where Jacobsen designed an employee lunchroom and terrace. At the SAS House similar sets of piers supported the hotel tower, framing the main entrance to the lobby and enclosing the elevator vestibule on the lower two floors.

The glass curtain walls that enclosed the office floors of the Jespersen House were constructed of laminated wood sections that were bolted to the reinforced-concrete floors and covered in bent aluminum sheets. Within this grid, operable windows and spandrels of dark green glass formed tight surfaces facing east and west. Jacobsen's hand is evident throughout, most obviously in the choice of the dark green glass, but even more so in the rigorous system of proportions, which was based on the golden section and a progression of squares. Stone is used to clad the service tower, which contains the elevator, stairs, and toilets. Applied in a grid of vertical units, the stone is treated as equal to the glass in texture and dimensions.

The Jespersen House may have served as a structural model for the hotel tower, but the development of the SAS's curtain wall would depend on the precedent of Rødovre Town Hall. Jacobsen was awarded the job following a competition in 1954. Using an innovative system of precast concrete beams and planks, the build-ing was completed two years later. As has often been noted, the overall form of the town hall and the module of the curtain wall were derived from Eero Saarinen's buildings at the General Motors Technical Center, completed outside of Detroit in 1952. Both men were developing the structural and formal language of Mies van der Rohe; Rødovre Town Hall offered ample testimony to the possibility of transforming industrial construction into an individual artistic statement. Jacobsen's building, through the refinement of detail and his ongoing exploration of interior transparency, lighting techniques, and modular construction, ultimately stands on its own merits. In the delicacy of its cladding, it surpasses the model.

The town hall consists of a three-story building containing offices and public services and a detached pavilion, with the council chamber and meeting rooms, that is linked to the main building by a glazed passageway. Both volumes were clad in continuous walls of glass, with end walls of dark Solvåg stone. But Jacobsen set them at a right angle to each other, creating a continuous interplay between transparency and opacity. As at the Jespersen building, glass and stone were treated as equivalent materials that vary in opacity and pattern. The correspondence between materials is made explicit by the identical dimensions of the translucent glass spandrels and the stone tiles. While the facades of the Jespersen building had relied on contrasts of transparency within a shallow assembly for visual power, the more sophisticated walls at Rødovre used the layering of material inherent in steel construction to create a textured surface of color and light.

↓
Jespersen House, Copenhagen, 1952–55.
At this small office building a few blocks
from Vesterbrogade, Jacobsen constructed
his first multistory glass wall. Operable
wood windows alternated with spandrel
panels of dark green glass to produce a
shimmering screen of reflected and inci-
dent light. The concrete service core, containing stairs, elevators, and toilets, was
covered with tiles of polished Solvag stone
aligned with the wall structure.

The long walls of the three-story office building were covered in bands of glass that reinforced its horizontal form. Along the west wall, facing the council chamber, the pattern of windows and spandrels was interrupted by a three-story atrium with an open stair and glazed elevators. One-by-two-meter insulated glass windows were suspended between the steel mullions that were bolted to the concrete structure at one-meter centers. Spandrel panels of tinted gray glass were held above and below the windows in delicate steel frames attached to the mullions with welded angles. An air space separated the spandrels from the insulation and captured the shadows cast by the projecting mullions. This sense of depth was heightened by the contrasts of color and surface finish: The steel assemblies containing the spandrel glass were painted a matte dark gray, while the mullions were protected by stainless steel covers that, in concert with the drip edges above and below the windows, created a web of reflected light.

The curtain wall of the SAS House combined the atmospheric effect of the Stelling House with the technical experience that Jacobsen gained at the Jespersen House and the Rødovre Town Hall: The Stelling House provided the model for an iridescent surface that changed color according to shifts in sunlight; the effect of the broad windows at the Jespersen House led the architect to diminish the proportion of transparent glass in his subsequent curtain walls; and the vertical rhythm of reflected light and the soft color of the spandrels at Rødovre provided the basis for the continuous surface of the tower walls.

Jacobsen and his staff later applied the lessons of the SAS House to a range of projects, built and unbuilt, including the headquarters of the Hamburg Electrical Works, the competition-winning scheme for a commercial complex, Industri Hus (Industry House), on Copenhagen's Town Hall square, and the National Bank of Denmark. Of these projects, it was the National Bank that absorbed the bulk of Jacobsen's energy in his final years and represented his final refinement of the curtain wall.

In 1961, a limited competition was organized to select an architect for the bank's new headquarters on a sensitive site along the Holmen Canal of Copenhagen's inner harbor. Because the site was occupied by existing bank offices and the printing works for the Danish mint, phased construction was necessary. Jacobsen's winning scheme was built between 1966 and 1978, though he lived to see the completion of only the first phase in 1971, a few weeks before his sudden death.

Jacobsen's design combined a single-story plinth that occupied the entire block with a five-story office building along the eastern edge of the site. Set on a continuous base of Porsgruun marble, the office block is supported on columns that allow sunlight to filter through high windows at the top of the perimeter wall. While the endwalls and plinth are solid planes of marble, the long walls are clad in gray bronze, a contrast of materials that recalled Rødovre Town Hall. A repetitive bay structure that tied the contrasting materials together was applied along all four walls, creating a visual echo of the surrounding seventeenth- and

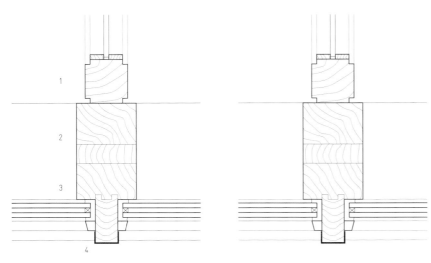

↑
Detail plan of curtain wall, Jespersen House, 1:5. Industrialized building technology arrived late in Denmark, and Jacobsen used beams of laminated wood to produce the framing system for the Jespersen walls. The outer edges of the timber members were clad in bent aluminum profiles to give the appearance of a metal structure.

1 Glazed interior partition
2 Built-up timber mullion
3 Insulated window
4 Aluminum cover

→→
Typical office floor of the Jespersen House. Jacobsen carried the module and the transparency of the exterior glazing into the partitions of the office floors.

↓
View of Jespersen House facade. An eight-story office building for the construction firm of A. Jespersen and Sons allowed Jacobsen to create the first of a series of suspended glass walls that would transform his buildings into prisms of light and layered surfaces.

↘↘
Fire stair of the Jespersen House. The fire stair at the end of the corridor emerged from the building in a cylinder of glass, which continued to the basement. The juxtaposition of the structural pier and the glass cylinder was typical of Jacobsen's contrasts between solidity and weightless transparency. The cantilevered steel stair and delicate railing reiterate the structure of the building in miniature.

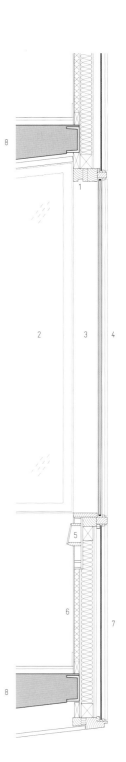

→
Wall section, Jespersen House, 1:20. The timber framework was hung from the edges of the concrete floor slabs, and the interior paneling featured integrated channels for electrical and telephone systems.

1 Built-up timber muntin
2 Glazed interior partition
3 Built-up timber mullion
4 Insulated window
5 Electrical wiring
6 Painted plywood panel
7 Opaque glass spandrel
8 Concrete floor slab

↓
Rødovre Town Hall, Rødovre, 1952–56. The
town hall was composed of a pair of
simple prisms—a three-story office building and a one-story council chamber—
connected by a glass passageway. The
ninety-meter-long walls of the office
building were covered in a web of steel
with transparent, gray spandrels. Behind
the council chamber, the horizontal bands
of gray glass were interrupted by the
stair hall that extended the height of the
building.

→
Rødovre Town Hall. The town hall buildings used contrasting materials arranged at a right angle to create a constantly changing experience of transparency and opacity. On the end walls of the council chamber, the module of the curtain wall was enlarged to create glass screens that reinforced the public nature of the council meetings. On one end of the office structure, a large clock with an etched glass screen linked the building to town halls of the past.
↓
Rødovre Town Hall. The end walls of the council chamber were covered in black Solvag marble, a stone that Jacobsen prized for its subtle patterns of iridescent mica. The town emblem of a rampant bull was etched into the stone.

Section of curtain wall, Rødovre Town Hall, 1:20. The cantilevered beams were connected by a low concrete curb that supported the insulated parapet wall. In front of this parapet, two panels of transparent gray-tinted glass were held in steel frames welded to the vertical members.

1 Vinyl tile over acoustic insulation
2 Precast concrete floor slab
3 Wood beam ceiling with acoustic ceiling tiles
4 Painted wood paneling
5 Insulated window
6 8-mm translucent glass spandrel

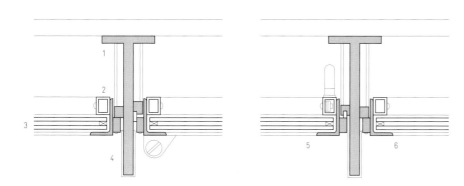

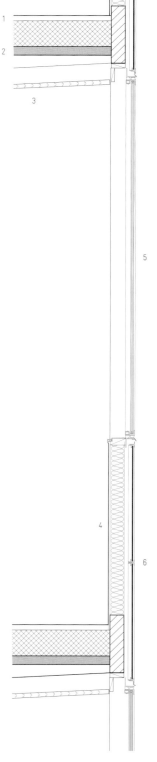

Plan detail of curtain wall, 1:5. T-shaped steel mullions were the basis for a delicate assemblage of angles that held layers of glass and insulation in parallel planes. The pocket between these planes captured shadows cast through the transparent panels.

1 Steel mullion with welded angle frames
2 Aluminum glass stop
3 Insulated glass
4 Stainless steel mullion cap
5 Operable window
6 Fixed window

Details of the curtain wall. The stone panels that covered the ends of the office building corresponded to the height of the gray glass panels. The mullions and drip edges below the windows were covered in stainless steel.

eighteenth-century buildings. Jacobsen had originally envisioned the curtain wall as a series of gray-tinted windows with dark-gray spandrels. Instead, the monumental bay windows were built as a double-wall system with a continuous outer layer of bronze-colored, heat-resistant glass and an inner, operable unit of clear glass. At the corners of each bay, the inverted L-shaped mullion developed for the Royal Hotel reinforced the effect of an assemblage of vertical leaves. A band of opaque, dark-gray glass at the top of each bay conceals mechanical equipment and creates the visual weight of a cornice.

Jacobsen cultivated surface treatments as a means of architectural expression. Traditionally, architectural ornament has served two purposes: to cover joints and hide the imperfections of craftwork, and to add visual emphasis and enliven plain materials. Jacobsen eschewed applied ornament, but he used pattern and texture to imbue his forms and spaces with visual richness. In the end, he found an industrial vehicle for his aesthetic tendencies in the mass-produced curtain wall. His development of glass walls and his use of polished stone tiles, which were embedded with shards of mica and fossilized marine life, were exterior equivalents of the wood veneers and patterned curtains he used to line his buildings.

Aerial view of central Copenhagen. The new National Bank building occupied an entire block along the Holmens Canal of Copenhagen's inner harbor. Jacobsen's competition-winning scheme combined a traditional perimeter block with a modern office structure. The six-story building was constructed atop a plinth that contained the parking facilities and a series of basements for currency printing and storage. By placing the bulk of the building along the east edge of the site, Jacobsen strengthened the street wall of Niels Jules Gade, while enhancing the views of the Holmens Church and the multispired Stock Exchange.

National Bank of Denmark, Copenhagen, 1961–78. The vertical bays, clad in Porsgruun marble and aluminum curtain walls of gray bronze glass, repeated the structural module of the surrounding masonry buildings. Between the low wall of the plinth and the body of the office block, recessed skylights channeled light into the windowless first floor.

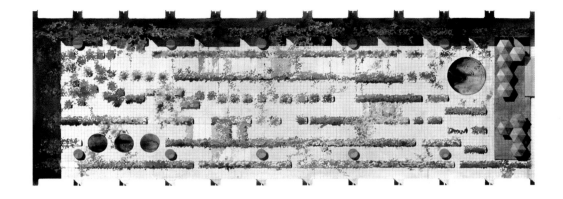

Watercolor of the roof gardens for the National Bank of Denmark, 1961. Jacobsen's entry to the competition for the bank included this plan for a garden at the center of the office block. At one end of the paving, a platform with tables and umbrellas would provide the staff with a small terrace.

↓
Roof gardens. At the center of the building, a pair of planted roofs with skylights for the print hall below created views for the surrounding offices. The gardens' dark glass walls with their taut surfaces and slender proportions represented Jacobsen's most classical treatment of the modernist curtain wall.

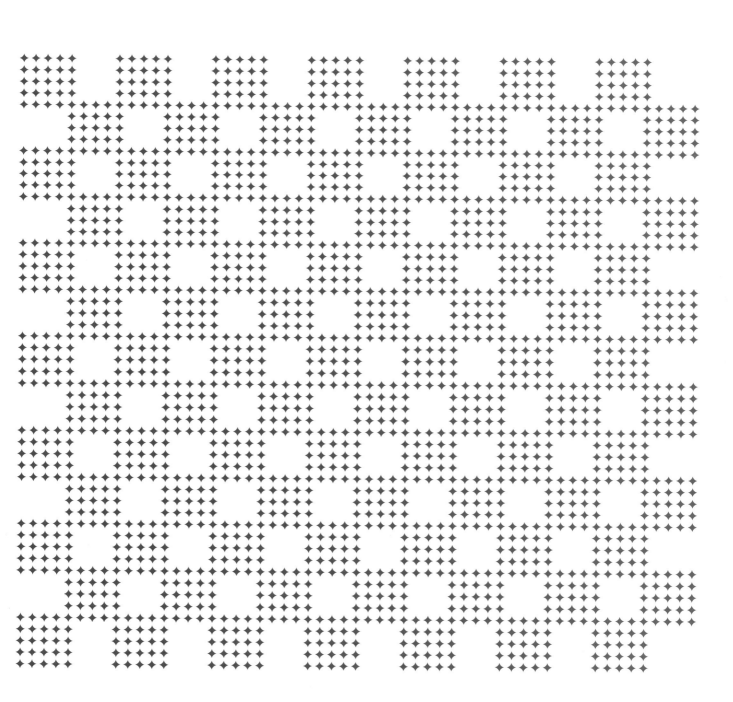

Artificial lighting was a central feature of Jacobsen's interior land-scapes. At the SAS House, he introduced an array of new fixtures, including a series of unique installations, that suited the diverse programs and spaces in the multi-use building. In Room 606, a trio of these lamps, stationary and mobile, represent the constellation of lights designed for the building. Their varied forms and architectural roles, from built-in fixture to freestanding object, reflected Jacobsen's treatment of lighting as both substance and object.

In one corner of the room stands a Royal floor lamp, the signature design for the hotel. While the standard model was finished in dark brown enamel, 606 is furnished with the special model created for the hotel suites, with a blue base and a chrome-plated stem that reflects light and reduces the lamp's visual weight. Its corresponding ellipses of base and shade, connected by an off-set stem, create an illuminated counterpart to the suspended shells and steel legs of the room's furniture. Above the cast-iron base, the slender steel tube supports a shade of burlap reinforced with a translucent plastic lining. The woven shell served as a portable version of the porous curtains Jacobsen used throughout the hotel to diffuse light and connect disparate spaces. A pair of incandescent bulbs is controlled by a three-way switch, allowing varied levels of illumination, from ambient source to reading lamp.

A pair of Eklipta (Discus) lamps hang just below the ceiling at opposite ends of the room. The Eklipta was originally designed as a wall and ceiling fixture for Town Hall; these round ellipses of white glass project a corona of light onto the adjacent surfaces, softening the contrast between shade and support. Outfitted with either single or dual bulbs, the Eklipta was used throughout the Royal Hotel guest rooms to provide pools of light that created a background to the movable reading lamps.

↑

Room 606, Royal Hotel, SAS House, Copenhagen, 1955–60. Jacobsen supplemented
natural light with a series of cylindrical
lamps in glass and plastic, creating
a fluid constellation of hovering objects.
Combining built-in fixtures and freestanding lamps, his lighting designs for
the SAS House used both ambient and
focused illumination to produce a range
of intimate and distinctive spaces.

→

Room 606. The vestibule between the
corridor and bedroom is lit by a single
disk of molded glass and is finished in
wood paneling painted in glossy pigments
to make the most of the available light.
On the left, built-in closets contain drawers and hanging space. Below the closets,
deep coves finished with durable wenge
strips provide space for luggage storage.

↓

Study for the Eklipta ceiling lamp, 1958.
The Eklipta lamp uses a forty-five-
centimeter wide shade of white glass to
create a floating disk that projects light in
all directions and prevents harsh contrast
with the ceiling. A recessed junction box
allows the fixture with two sixty-watt
bulbs to hover just below the ceiling.

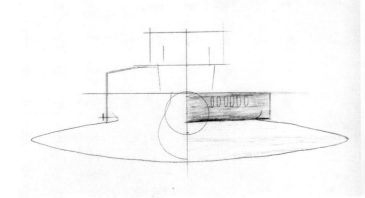

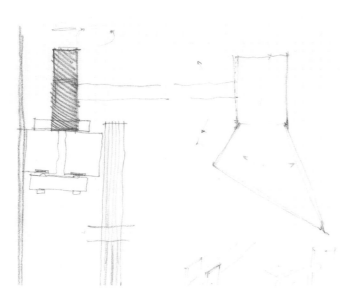

↑

Room 606. Above the beds, a pair of sliding lamps allow guests to adjust the lighting according to their individual needs. The lamps contain twenty-five-watt bulbs and focus light through a steel tube. Cylindrical shades of gray and white Plexiglas direct light against the walls and prevent glare. Additional reading lamps are mounted in the paneling at the opposite end of the room. By building the lamps into the woodwork, Jacobsen maximized available space and allowed the cantilevered tables to be rearranged.

←

Study for the reading lamp, 1958. Jacobsen had originally planned to create reading lamps with flaired metal shades. This sketch for a prototype closely resembles the wall-mounted Visor lamps that were installed in the SAS air terminal.

Above the wenge paneling, pairs of cylindrical reading lamps are mounted in a continuous slot that allows them to slide to any position along the length of the walls. An innovative accordion cable provides continuous power as the fixtures move, while a plexiglass shade prevents glare. These sliding lamps complete the system of repositionable furnishings that allowed the rooms to be reconfigured to suit the needs of the guests. Jacobsen's first sketch for the lamps includes an early version of the Visor shade, which would be developed as a set of multipurpose fixtures and used throughout the public areas of the building. A prototypical guest room exhibited in Paris in 1958 displayed the Visors above an early version of the wall-hung cabinets, converted for the occasion into showcases for Jacobsen's new flatware. Whether for reasons of economy or formal variation, Jacobsen abandoned the rail-mounted Visor and developed the reading lamp fixture instead.

→
View of the SAS House from across
Vesterbrogade. This view captures the variety of lighting strategies that Jacobsen
used in the building. The ground floor was
illuminated with dramatic contrasts of
light and shadow, surrounded by a continuous border of backlit signage. On the
second floor, individual fixtures created
ambient light, while a grid of skylights
punctured the structure's roof. In the guest
rooms light was used sparingly, and
through the windows the bright forms of
the ceiling and floor lamps are visible.

At the base of the SAS House, Jacobsen created two of the most dramatic interiors of the twentieth century: the passenger hall of the SAS air terminal and the lobby of the Royal Hotel. Throughout the ground floor, Jacobsen blended natural and artificial light from a variety of sources to create a pair of opposing settings. Above the orderly rows of seating in the double-height passenger hall, a diffusing skylight provided an even, shadowless light that created a single, clear open space. The lobby of the Royal Hotel, by contrast, was a shadowy zone of indistinct boundaries, punctuated by pools of light and filled with reflective surfaces. Daylight was admitted through the walls of glass that wrapped the street fronts of the building, which also acted as vitrines for the airline and the shops that enclosed the lobby. Jacobsen recessed the storefronts in order to heighten the showcase effect, which also created an overhang to shelter pedestrians in inclement weather.

A broad skylight set into the roof illuminates the passenger hall as well as a portion of the hotel lobby with diffused sunlight. Built-in fixtures and luminous ceilings along the edges of the twin halls created pools of warm fluorescent light that supplemented the natural light. A series of fixtures designed especially for the building provided pools of warm incandescent light at points of repose and served as small-scale sculptural decoration. Like most of the fixtures in the building, these illuminated sculptures displayed Jacobsen's penchant for minimal form and apparent weightlessness. The combination of overlapping vistas and suspended fixtures produced a sense of disembodied experience that suited both the function and the location of the building.

The first phase of the SAS House was completed in the summer of 1959 with the air terminal. Following the model of a railroad station, the air terminal was organized around a two-story passenger hall with service counters and ticket agents on the periphery and staff offices on a mezzanine level. Between the hall's skylight and luminous ceiling, a battery of fluorescent lamps assured a constant level of illumination regardless of the hour or the season. Beneath this artificial sky, layers of glass and wood framed porous boundaries that reinforced the sense of perspective in the hall while allowing light to filter in from the periphery.

A check-in counter and baggage rooms along the west edge of the hall were flanked by arrival and departure gates leading to buses in the parking lot. At the south end of the room, an elegant stair of steel and glass gave travelers access to a range of services. Downstairs, men's and women's hairdressers, a children's playroom, and a darkened rest area catered to both compressed and extended itineraries. At the top of the stair, overlooking the hall, a freestanding bar provided a meeting point while allowing the patrons to remain aware of the comings and goings below.

A row of telephones located beneath the bar was illuminated by Jacobsen's Visor wall lamps, which consisted of rounded steel shades mounted on a steel stem. The fixtures could also be used as desk or floor lamps, a versatility brought about by an integrated hinge at the junction

↑
Bar area in the passenger hall. At the top of the stair, a freestanding platform framed with glass panels and covered in blue gray linoleum contained a bar with a panoramic view of the hall. In the corners of the hall, freestanding columns and panels of wenge and ash created a composition of abstract forms.

→
View of the passenger hall from the bar. Even lighting delivered through the translucent glass ceiling and a simple plan resulted in a passenger hall characterized by its clarity and functionality. Jacobsen used contrasting woods to reinforce the axial symmetry and extensive areas of glass to allow an intuitive grasp of the layout and prevent a sense of enclosure. In front of the mezzanine that housed staff offices, broad panels of ash reflected the light from above. At either end of the hall, walls of dark wenge drew the eye to the bar and the bank. The structural columns were treated as independent elements that provided a spatial rhythm and loosely defined the seating area.

↓
View of the SAS air terminal's passenger hall from under the bar. At one end of the room, a stair of steel and glass provided access to the services located in the basement and the bar that overlooked the hall. On the left, a wall of ash panels and glass transoms separated the hall from the bus depot in the parking lot. On the opposite wall, full-height windows overlooked the Hammerichsgade.

↓
Public telephones in the passenger hall.
Below the bar, public telephones were enclosed in sheets of tempered glass and
perforated metal screens that absorbed
sound. Projecting out over the stainless
steel counter, the smooth shades of the
Visor lamps contrasted with the wenge
panels. The bent-metal shade was the
basis for a series of fixtures that included
the floor and table lamps displayed at the
Musée des Arts Décoratifs in 1958.

→
Newsstand in the passenger hall.
Jacobsen designed a circular newsstand
with graduated shelving that would
display a range of magazines in the
smallest possible space.
↓
Bank in the passenger hall. Detailed as a
floating object between walls of glass and
hovering wood, a bank and currency
exchange was located between the passenger hall and the travel agency, serving
both areas.
↘
Travel agency in the passenger hall.
Domestic travel arrangements were
handled by a pair of service counters at
the north end of the agency. The counters
were lit by a luminous surface that
continued the paneling grid and provided
a bright contrast to the higher, gray
green ceiling. Signs were treated as free-
floating elements independent of the
architectural surfaces.

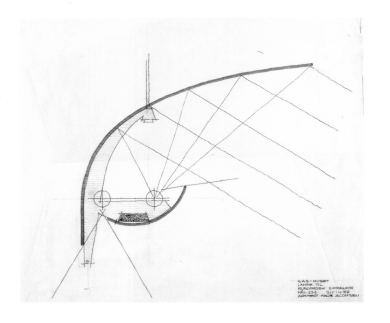

←
Study for the travel agency fixture. This sketch depicts a pair of tubular lamps that provide both direct and reflected light. The nested brass sheets directed rays onto the service counter while preventing a view of the source from either side. This detailed attention to comfort was evident in the hundreds of pieces of equipment and furniture that were designed for the airline staff.

↓
Travel agency in the SAS air terminal. In the center of the travel agency, a freestanding structure provided bookings for European destinations. The service counters were lit by two rows of cylindrical fluorescent lamps that reflected light from a pair of curved brass sheets. The inner and outer shades were connected by steel tubes that also contained the wiring.

between the two pieces that allowed the shade to rotate. In the desk and floor Visors installed in the hotel suites and staff offices, the asymmetrical profile of the hood was echoed by the angle of the stem as it met a heavy metal base, where a circular cutout repeats the mouth of the shade. This development of a single form suited to varied uses was a recurring theme in Jacobsen's work and reflected his desire to distill his formal vocabulary to a handful of basic shapes and materials.

At the north end of the hall, opposite the bar, a branch of the Kobenhavn Handelsbank was set into the wall of glass that led to the travel and car rental agencies at the end of the building. Parallel service counters allowed the bank to function in both directions, providing currency exchange for tourists in the passenger hall and expediting purchases in the travel agency. The agency itself was divided into separate areas for domestic, continental, and intercontinental itineraries. A large island in its center, where tickets for European travel were issued, was lit by one of several custom fixtures that combined modular construction and specific lighting requirements.

Suspended from the ceiling in parallel rows, these delicate metal fixtures used a pair of aluminum reflectors to provide continuous light to the countertop while shielding both traveler and agent from glare. The smaller interior reflector was suspended on curved, chrome-plated steel tubes that carried the electrical wiring and supported a fluorescent lamp at both of its ends. Within the outer reflector, a steel rod intersected the suspension tubes and was tied back to a thin steel wire that stabilized the entire assembly.

Along the edges of the agency, service areas for overseas and domestic travel were treated as niches, with suspended ceilings of glass that repeated the lighting strategy of the passenger hall. While intercontinental excursions were handled at a row of staggered desks, the counter for domestic travel was a finely detailed piece of cabinetry that featured wenge panels cut across the grain for decorative effect.

On 1 July 1960, the SAS Royal Hotel was formally opened by the queen and king of Denmark, who played host to a group of dignitaries accommodated on the eight floors of the tower that were complete. Construction of the remaining twelve floors, the restaurant, and the cocktail bar would be finished by December. The street fronts were already wrapped with shops catering to hotel guests and to the pedestrian public. The prime frontage, along Vesterbrogade, was reserved for a cornucopia of Danish crafts and luxury goods. At the intersection with Hammerichsgade, the Art Royal boutique, a joint venture of the Royal Copenhagen porcelain factory and Georg Jensen silversmiths, displayed the most traditional of Danish handicrafts in an absolutely contemporary setting. Further west, Berger Christensen displayed the fur garments that had earned it a royal warrant, and a parfumerie sold precious scents. Along Hammerichsgade, a series of shops provided gifts and souvenirs for the hotel guests.

The shops were the initial evidence of Jacobsen's practice of method design: Rather than

Entry to the Royal Hotel. Along Hammerichsgade, a projecting canopy with an abstract crown marked the entrance to the hotel lobby. The walls of the third floor, the junction between podium and tower, were recessed sheets of glass that articulated the division between the horizontal and vertical blocks.

Entry vestibule. The structural piers of the hotel tower framed the entry vestibule. This view from the elevator lobby illustrates the use of glass to heighten the connection to the street. The vestibule ceiling and the entrance canopy were suspended from the structural slab, allowing light to filter through the gaps and promote the effect of an indistinct boundary.

acting as a barrier between interior and exterior, the storefronts extended the materials and lighting of the lobby out to the sidewalk. Within the shops, partitions and service counters were covered in the same system of wenge paneling that lined the lobby and the air terminal. After devising a typeface and signage system that would suit all the areas of the ground floor, Jacobsen designed each of the shops as a museum-quality exhibition, lavishing his customary attention to detail on the merchandising requirements of each business. Above all, he sought a uniform presentation; the storefronts used recessed lighting and hanging displays to present their wares, whether porcelain bowls or cans of pipe tobacco. To eliminate visual obstructions between sidewalk and lobby, much of the merchandise was presented on glass shelves suspended on steel cables. Below eye level, low tables provided platforms for meticulous arrangements of objects.

The entrance to the Royal Hotel sat beneath a cantilevered canopy surmounted with an abstract crown and was framed by a pair of enormous piers clad in richly veined black marble. Inside, in a deliberate contrast to the system of grids that permeated the building, Jacobsen lit the hotel lobby with varied levels of illumination that concentrated light at key points and created cues for movement and rest. The ceiling was comprised of dark green steel acoustic tiles perforated by hundreds of recessed incandescent lamps. The lobby floor was paved in a light gray Porsgruun marble from western Norway that held the light from the overhead lamps. The wenge paneling created dark edges that, in concert with the irregular patterns of light, resulted in a room of indistinct size. Around the edges of this shadowy hall, Jacobsen created a series of lower, brightly lit volumes that contained specialized functions.

Just inside the hotel's vestibule, a pool of light illuminated a trio of large blue-and-gray carpets furnished with the Egg chairs and sofas Jacobsen had developed for the rooms. A white bar of light suspended above the reception desk, just beyond the seating area, was the brightest object in the room, leading guests to their initial destination. The fixture was made of sheet metal and steel angles, the chain of staggered planes projected light above and below, its glowing edges softening its form. In its pattern and in its manipulation of depth, the fixture recalls Jacobsen's early studies for the exterior of the tower and reflects his preoccupations with pattern and seriality.

A second pair of piers directly across from the entrance, clad in the same marble, framed the elevator vestibule. This brightly lit recess, similar to the travel agencies of the air terminal, was paneled in oak. A louvered ceiling with concealed fluorescent lamps illuminated the oak, creating a warm box of light. To one side, four high-speed elevators connected the lobby to the dining level one floor above and to the guest rooms in the tower. The elevator cabs were treated as pieces of cabinetry, with doors and interiors of wenge that presaged the wood linings of the guest rooms.

Interior elevations, Royal Hotel lobby, 1960, 1:200. A set of freehand drawings show the modular surfaces of wood and glass that lined the interior walls of the lobby and the use of the shop windows as decorative elements. The wood paneling on the lower floors of the building was divided into 1.2-meter widths, a subdivision of the 4.8-meter column grid that supported the podium. This modular system of construction allowed Jacobsen to align different materials with flush surfaces and precise joints. Glass doors and display windows conformed to the widths of the woodwork. The shopwindows were sketched with displays of floating objects that acted as an additional filter between the interior and the street.

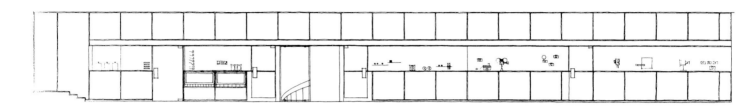

→

South wall, along Vesterbrogade. Opposite the stair and winter garden, the short, continuous glass wall of the lobby was equipped with a trio of full-height display cases and pivoting doors. Above the glass, the wenge panels contained horizontal grills for ventilation. The glass doors allowed views of the street and, in combination with the shallow showcases, produced a juxtaposition of interior and exterior that fused lobby and shop into a unified space.

↙ ↓

East wall, along Hammerichsgade.
On either side of the entry vestibule, the
structural piers of the hotel tower were
clad in panels of black marble arranged in
a running bond pattern. The shops that
bracketed the entry displayed a wide
range of gifts and souvenirs. Wenge paneling above the display windows was
aligned with the ceiling of the vestibule.

Below the windows, the panels extended
to the level of the built-in shelves in each
shop, while pivoting glass doors provided
access from the lobby. At the far end of
the wall, a short flight of steps led to the
air terminal, allowing guests to enter the
hotel directly from the passenger hall.

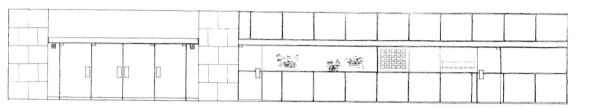

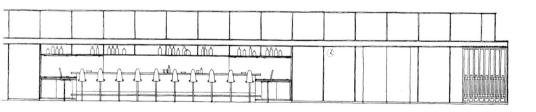

↖ ↑

West wall. Opposite the newsstand and
flowershop, the reception desks were
aligned with the paneling module and lit
by a long fixture of alternating metal
planes. Next to the reception counters, a
marble-clad box contained the elevator
lobby with four high-speed cars that
stopped at the second floor before continuing to the guest rooms in the hotel tower.

In the snack bar, a row of stools faced a
bronze counter and back-lit display of
bottles that hovered above the windows
to the kitchen. Beyond the bar, the paneling continued to the firewall between
hotel and air terminal, where wooden
screens defined a row of booths facing
the winter garden.

Window display of the Art Royal boutique in the Royal Hotel. The edges of the hotel lobby were defined by spotlit arrays of merchandise. The cashwrap counters and solid partitions continued the dominating wenge paneling that lined the lobby.

Exterior view of the Art Royal boutique. This flagship shop was a joint venture of the Royal Copenhagen porcelain works and the Georg Jensen silversmiths. Goods from both companies were arranged in a series of dramatic presentations. The use of free-hanging curtains as room dividers would reappear throughout the building.

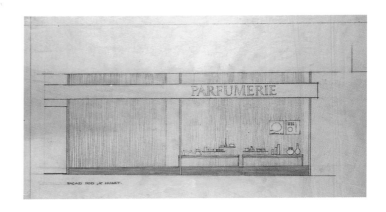

↑
Study for the perfume shop, 1959. Jacobsen's designs for the individual shops were united by the use of floating shelves and low tables. The suspended displays allowed each piece to be seen as a sculptural object subordinate to the architecture.

→

Detail of the Royal Hotel reception fixture.
The 8.7-meter-long linear pendant was
constructed of steel sheets painted in
white enamel and welded into a chain
of alternating planes. The overlapping
squares resemble Jacobsen's initial
studies for the hotel curtain wall.

↘

Sections of the reception fixture, 1:10.
Four perpendicular planes of steel were
connected by welded tabs and rectangles,
forming boxes that concealed forty-watt
bulbs. Another series of bulbs placed
alternatingly between these boxes were
concealed behind steel planes that were
welded to the fixture and let light through
on all sides.

↓ ↘

Lobby and reception desk. The hotel lobby
was a twenty-nine-by-sixteen-meter
single room with a Porsgruun marble floor
and a carefully controlled mixture of
natural and artificial light. Set into the
4.8-meter-high ceiling of dark green metal
panels, strings of recessed reflectors
created irregular pools of light. The bright
fixture above the reception desk created
the effect of a floating sculpture.

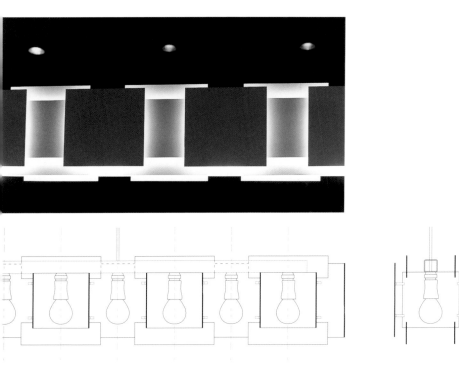

Longitudinal Section   Cross Section

→

View of the Royal Hotel lobby. Jacobsen
used artificial light to heighten the sense
of spatial variety within the expansive hall
of the lobby. At the south end of the room,
dense lines of recessed spotlights illuminated the seating groups in front of the
reception desk. Along the edges of the
hall, spot-lit displays of flowers, silver,
and furs from the shops created a background of shapes and textures akin to
a three-dimensional wall covering. Reflected in the glass doors and marble of
the tower piers, the fixture above the reception desk appears as a disembodied
bar of light.

Much of the lobby's sensational effect lay in Jacobsen's inversion of the usual treatment of floor and ceiling. The light gray marble paving was the lightest and most reflective surface in the lobby, while the dark ceiling resembled an abstract night sky. Between these two contrasting planes, walls of wood and glass created alternating edges of reflection and pattern. The wall panels were framed by the diffused light coming through the shop windows. Backlit by day and top-lit at any hour by dozens of point fixtures, the storefront displays created a virtual wallpaper of suspended objects. In an effect that recalled the textiles that had preoccupied Jacobsen since the 1940s, the merchandise became a part of the interior surface of the lobby, furthering the dissolution of spatial boundaries.

The focal point of the lobby was a spiral stair, six meters in diameter, which led up to the restaurant and a series of lounges on the second floor. Jacobsen treated the stair like a sculptural object that was hung from steel rods anchored in the floor and ceiling above. The steps were steel plates welded together into a continuous ribbon and painted white to reflect light from the winter garden. On their top surface, a swath of olive green carpet cascaded down from the second floor, stopping just above the gray marble. This welded steel ring received all of its structural support from above and Jacobsen was able to expose the edges of the steps and display the thin plates of tread and riser. Just above the steps, standing free of the suspension rods, a series of posts and a continuous steel railing held panels of gray Plexiglas that continued in the balustrade overhead.

Beyond the stair lay a double-height winter garden that served as a sitting room and provided a respite from the activity of the reception area. Lit from above by a glass ceiling, this interior courtyard was enclosed in walls of glass and wrapped with open-weave curtains that heightened the sense of enclosure and softened the contrast with the surrounding hall. On the long sides of the room, freestanding columns were encased in walls of glass that created two-story vitrines, 1.2 meters deep, which were filled with scores of hanging orchids. Suspended from above on steel cables, the flowers bore an unmistakable resemblance to the hanging displays of merchandise along the edges of the lobby. Dark brown deep-pile Rya carpets alongside these vitrines anchored groups of Pot chairs and rosewood tables and complemented the textures of the floor-level plantings.

A pair of glass doors to one side of the winter garden led to the snack bar, which seated seventy patrons in a pair of distinctive settings. Parallel to the flower wall, a bar faced in panels of wenge and bronze was lined with stools that faced the kitchen window and a backlit bottle display. A suspended ceiling of oak strips and recessed lamps above the bar created a plane of warm light. Additional seating was provided along the back of the winter garden in rows of tables that paralleled the firewall between the hotel and air terminal.

Jacobsen's recurring motif of abstracted nature appeared in the alcoves, framed by oak

Royal Hotel winter garden. At the north end of the lobby, a 120-square-meter glass box connected the first and second floors. The two-story vitrine walls were filled with orchids, fusing Jacobsen's devotion to nature and transparency into a single episode. Above the translucent glass ceiling, a battery of fluorescent lamps, serviced by a special rolling trolley, provided even illumination throughout the day and night.

← Detail of the winter garden. Double-glass walls, 1.2 meters apart, created vitrines in which columns and flora were treated as sculptural forms suspended between floor and skylight. The hues and textures of the flowers were repeated in the bed of plantings that covered the vitrine floor.

↓ Winter garden looking into the snack bar. The flower walls of the winter garden were interior versions of the lobby shops and created a series of dramatic juxtapositions. With sets of transparent screens, the lobby combined a series of distinctive settings with a sense of continuous space.

→ Entrance to the snack bar. A pivoting glass door provided entrance to the snack bar, where Jacobsen's distinctive plywood stools were covered in chestnut brown leather. The glass partition was treated as a floating plane that corresponded to the module of the continuous paneling.

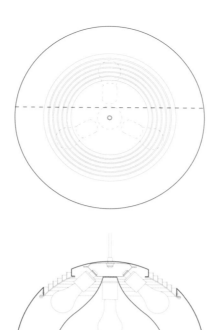

Plan and section, AJ Royal pendant, 1:10. Concentric steel shells separated a trio of forty-watt incandescent bulbs from a seventy-five-watt silver reflector. The mixture of ambient and directed light typified Jacobsen's nuanced approach to lighting design.

↓

Snack bar. At the end of the bar, rows of tables provided seating for groups of diners. Along the firewall to the air terminal, a row of booths was defined by a dropped ceiling of oak latticework and matching screens that created an interior arbor.

atticework, that served as urbane arbors gazing out toward the winter garden. The alcoves' oak screens were, in essence, wooden versions of the textiles that Jacobsen used throughout the hotel o subdivide large rooms into layers of nested, intimate spaces. The alcoves were lit by a pendant ixture, the AJ Royal, that combined Jacobsen's interest in reflected light with an evolving tendency toward platonic geometry. Within their hemispherical shell, an internal shade separated a trio of bulbs from a central, silver-coated bulb, creating round pools of direct and reflected ight and preventing a view of the light sources. At the top of the shell, concentric louvers allowed light to spill out of the top, emphasizing the rounded bowl of polished metal and providing gentle ambient light.

The ground floor of the SAS House was the culmination of Jacobsen's exercises in transparency and display. The habitable vitrines that lined the street fronts of the hotel were both a means of displaying merchandise to maximum effect and a vehicle for connecting very different environments through a filter of suspended objects. The sketches of the lobby walls, with their floating pipes and perfume bottles, and the actual displays that Jacobsen arranged illustrate his integration of commerce and architecture. The lobby winter garden that joined the public floors replicated this effect, with its walls of orchids, which were a living version of Jacobsen's earlier floral textiles.

↓

Parlor of the Rothenborg House, Klampenborg, 1929–30. Jacobsen's use of transparency to create interior landscapes can
be traced to the flower windows of his
early houses. In this parlor, a continuous
window planting trough juxtaposed cacti
and house plants against the exterior
foliage.

acobsen's development of transparent interiors can be traced in
series of buildings that began in the 1930s and spanned a wide
ange of functions. In the same manner that his work bridged the
oundaries between architecture and the applied arts, Jacobsen's
uildings tended to disregard conventional distinctions between
omestic and institutional settings. Unencumbered by precon-
eptions of what a house or a factory should look like, Jacobsen
eated each commission as an opportunity to develop a synthesis
f prosaic beauty and functional poetry that benefited residents
nd clerical workers alike. At the same time, his postwar single-
amily houses used modular construction and industrial building
echniques to exploit natural light and visual ties to the surround-
ng landscape. As a result of this cross-pollination, buildings with
astly different programs, from private homes to schools and
actories, share both formal resemblances and an attention
utility and comfort that is decidedly domestic. This domesticity
eflects Jacobsen's formative training designing small houses
the 1930s; and it was in these houses that his exploration of
ransparency began.

Jacobsen's early gardens had interior counterparts in the
lomstervindue, the flower windows that he developed for the
iving rooms of his single-family houses. Most often located on
corner room, these glass boxes allowed natural light to penetrate
eep into the house and juxtaposed cultivated nature against
he backdrop of a changing landscape. These interior gardens sig-
aled the beginning of a devotion to nature on Jacobsen's part that
would eventually fuse architecture and horticulture into a series
of constructed landscapes. The prototype for these layered compositions was the double window at the Wandel House, where an
otherwise traditional feature of northern European houses was filled
with potted plants. Two years later, while briefly under the spell of
Le Corbusier, Jacobsen designed the all-white concrete Rothenborg House with extensive horizontal windows. In the living room,
a corner window allowed light from two directions to nurture window planters and hanging pots and extended the house into the
surrounding woods.

After World War II, Jacobsen enlarged these *blomstervindue* to monumental scale at the Hårby School in his first step
toward an architecture of glass volumes. The school combined and
reinterpreted the gabled wings and staggered plans of Jacobsen's
domestic work on an institutional scale, with faculty housing and
a low wing for special classrooms organized around a central two-
story block containing classrooms and the assembly hall. The hall
was lit by the faceted glass boxes that combined window and skylight into a single prism and filled the room with even north light.

In the early 1950s, as Jacobsen's buildings grew in scale
and technical sophistication, load-bearing brick walls were supplanted by concrete frames with cantilevered floors wrapped in en-
velopes of glass. The interior walls of the buildings underwent a
corresponding transformation, becoming lightweight partitions
freely located on the open floors made possible by the modular
structures. With the Jespersen House and Rødovre Town Hall, even

Assembly hall of the Hårby School, Hårby (Fyn), 1948–50. The clerestory monitors filled the assembly hall with even, north light. The glass wall enclosing the staircase reflected the skylights and increased the apparent length of the hall. Beneath the mezzanine, a row of uplights suggests early versions of the Visor lamp.
↓
Watercolor of the Hårby School. This watercolor of the elementary school illustrates the enlargement of the flower window into a major architectural device. Along the eave of the main building, projecting glass boxes combined window and skylight in a row of monumental lanterns.

as he worked to develop carefully proportioned, elegantly detailed facades, Jacobsen filled the buildings with transparent walls, creating virtual prisms permeated with natural light. In both these buildings, he combined a double-loaded corridor, the most efficient form of circulation, with central rows of columns and cantilevered beams that tapered to the exterior walls. Beneath sloping ceilings, the interior walls were independent surfaces of glass and wood that could be repositioned to respond to the inhabitants' needs.

At the Jespersen House, offices were arranged on either side of a corridor that extended from the circulation core at the north end of the site. Partitions of wood enclosed the offices to desk height, while glass panes extended to the ceiling. A delicate steel stair descending from the suspended undercroft to the street reiterated the cantilevered structure of the building and received its own vitrine, a cylindrical glass case that served as a floating counterpoint to the enormous pillars that supported the building.

At Rødovre Town Hall, which accommodated more varied functions, the walls along the corridors had service windows in the double wall that contained ventilation ducts and a row of columns on the west side, and continuous glass transoms above the height of the doors on the east side that used the sloping ceilings to direct natural light to the spine of the building. While the offices of the Jespersen House would reappear in miniature form as the shops of the Royal Hotel, the freestanding columns and glass transoms of the town hall would be repeated throughout the SAS air terminal.

The direct precedent for these tapered structures was the showroom for Massey Harris, a manufacturer of farm equipment, that was completed in 1952 on Roskildevej, a busy highway west of Copenhagen. The building contained offices, an exhibition hall, and service facilities in a pair of offset buildings framed in concrete. Demonstrating the basic strategy that would be used at the Munkegård School and reappear in grander materials throughout the following decade, the building combined long surfaces of glass and steel with end walls of brick. The showroom itself applied the display techniques that Jacobsen had used in his offices and shops to the sale of machinery. It would be a simple transition from the display of tractors and combines along the highway to the jewelry and luxury goods along Vesterbrogade, ten years later.

Jacobsen's exploration of internal transparency and layered display in a domestic setting reached a climax at the Jürgensen House. This suburban house was the direct precedent for many of the features of the SAS House; the continuity across settings and building types serves to underline the synthetic quality of Jacobsen's best buildings.

The house for Rüthwen Jürgensen and his family was designed to produce overlapping views that joined dwelling and site into a continuous experience. The building was set on a plinth overlooking the Øresund and organized around an entry courtyard framed by a pair of wings, one containing a garage and suite for the parents, the other a row of bedrooms for the children. A central pavilion between the wings, parallel to the shoreline, extended the

→

Public stair, Rødovre Town Hall, 1952–56.
The public stair was a triumph of
engineering and craftsmanship. Five-
centimeter-thick steel bars were welded
and ground to create continuous stringers,
framing plate-steel treads covered with
linoleum and edged in stainless steel.
Sheets of tempered glass continued the
strategy of interior transparency and
created a microcosm of the building.

↙

Corridor, Rødovre Town Hall. The one-
meter module of the building structure
was carried through the interior partitions
and the ceiling panels. Along one side of
the central corridor, transoms allowed
light to filter into the passage, enhancing a
sense of orientation.

↓

Lobby, Rødovre Town Hall. Elevator, passage, and stair were combined in a set of
transparent planes that filled the hall with
layers of light and structure. In the center
of the lobby, the passageway to the council chamber was treated as an independent object that penetrated the three-story
window wall.

Massey-Harris showroom and offices, Glostrup, 1951–53. Along the wall facing the highway, the building was reduced to a frame covered with planes of glass that showcased the equipment. Tapered concrete beams were cantilevered from an interior wall to support a row of square bays. Between the principal columns, diagonal cables provided stability to the horizontal members and allowed the wall to resist wind loads. At night, fluorescent lamps at the top of the window wall bathed the implements in an even white light.

Site model of the Jürgensen House, Skodsborg, 1956. Jacobsen's private houses from the early 1950s typically combined a masonry base with a lightweight pavilion. This 400-square-meter house for a large family extended the strategy to create a paved plateau overlooking the Øresund. A trio of pavilions, framed in steel and covered with vertical siding, was arranged so that all the principal rooms received south light. The wing containing the parents' bedrooms was rotated to the south-east to take advantage of the views to the sea. The combination of an artificial topography and the interplay of transparent walls distinguish the Jürgensen House as one of Jacobsen's seminal buildings.
↓
Courtyard of the Jürgensen House. The three wings formed an entry courtyard with a low wall that sheltered a garden plot from the wind and created a prelude to the continuous windows of the central pavilion. The roof of the children's wing on the left was extended over the center wing to create a mezzanine that served as Jürgensen's library.

→
View of the dining room. From the dining room, the interior windows led the eye to the library at the top of the stairs. Linoleum floors and plaster partitions painted in warm colors gave the impression of a continuous room.
↓
Living and dining room. A sloping wood ceiling and interior windows reinforced the impression of a continuous room. On the left, domestic vitrines overlooking the courtyard were filled with collections of glass and porcelain. The living room was furnished with early versions of Series 3300 seating used in the SAS air terminal.

View from the living room of the Jürgensen House towards the Øresund. Along the east wall of the house, tall windows created expansive views of the sea. Beyond the windows, areas of glass block allowed daylight to filter into the basement. The terrace was covered in a grid of concrete pavers, fragmented by clusters of dark green moss. Beyond the terrace door, a winter garden received low light from two exposures and exterior stairs connected Jürgensen's library with the terrace.

sloping roof of the children's wing and contained the common areas of kitchen and dining and living rooms. Along the sides of this pavilion, between courtyard and coastline, Jacobsen created bands of windows that reflected the contrast between cultivated nature and the wildness of the sea. Facing back into the courtyard and extending the width of the wing, double-walled windows with glass shelves projected into the rooms and provided display for the artifacts and collections that the family had gathered. Full-height windows facing the sea extend to just above the floor, forming a foreground to the edge of the terrace. Above the height of the doors, continuous panes of glass created an internal perspective from stair to dining room. The sloping ceiling of wood planks and the painted surfaces above the line of the exterior windows highlight the equivalent role of windows and plinth as horizontal frames for the rolling landscape of slope and sea.

At the end of the living room, where the slope of the roof accommodated a second story, a steel stair ascended to Jürgensen's library and a balcony overlooking the sound. Below the library, set back from the window wall, a small, glass-enclosed winter garden provided a shaded setting for Jürgensen's collection of orchids. This terrarium was the direct inspiration for the winter garden running through the center of the SAS House.

Like any true connoisseur, Jacobsen realized the power of contrast, and his juxtapositions of the natural world and abstract form only serve to heighten the effect of both. In this sense, he was one of the truly organic architects of the twentieth century, displaying his veneration of nature by creating contrasting frameworks that highlight the uncontrollable and irregular character of the natural world. Throughout his work, walls between inside and outside, while detailed as crisply as possible, provided opportunities for collapsing the distance between foreground and background and reflected his formative years as a painter of landscapes.

Winter garden, Jürgensen House. Wooden
blinds sheltered a room-sized winter garden filled with Mr. Jürgensen's orchids.
The layered view from interior garden to
planted plinth to uncontrollable nature
encapsulated Jacobsen's essential idea
of architecture and landscape as a single
composition of juxtaposed scenes and
contrasting forms.

Section of living and dining rooms, Jürgensen House. The living and dining rooms were connected by interior transoms and a row of glass showcases that bracketed the doorway and projected into the rooms. Between the inner and outer panes of the glass showcase, a recessed track supported a natural wool curtain.

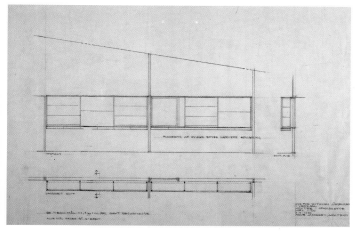

Detail of the showcase windows. The showcase windows contained glass shelves that displayed family heirlooms and domestic treasures. By including the family's possessions into the building, Jacobsen heightened the connection between nature and daily life and created a kaleidoscopic display of forms and colors.

↑
Room 606, Royal Hotel, SAS House,
Copenhagen, 1955–60. The wool curtain in
front of the twin beds allows the room to
be divided into sleeping and sitting areas.
At night, it is backlit to create a veil of
delicate texture akin to the wood paneling.

↓
Room 606. The curtains form a pleated
counterpart to the valance above the
window wall and complete Jacobsen's
composition of horizontal bands. A gray
carpet speckled with knots of pink and
white wool creates an animated plane
of shifting color.

The carpets and curtains Jacobsen designed for the Royal Hotel
were an integral part of the building. While modern architects generally left interior fabrics to others, treated them as separate from
their conceptions of space, or banished them altogether, Jacobsen
understood the role fabrics play in completing a room with texture
and detail. Depending on their location, the textiles in the hotel
served as thick coverings that complemented the irregular patterns
of wood and stone or as hanging screens that divided larger spaces
with veils of diffused light. The textiles in Room 606 fulfill both of
these roles and provide comfort as well as insight into Jacobsen's
use of color and pattern.

Jacobsen covered the upper floors of the hotel with broad-
loom carpets that absorbed sound and heightened the sense of
domestic ease. Rather than using solid colors, which would have
appeared monotonous and required constant vacuuming, Jacobsen
designed a series of subtle patterns that relied on the eye to blend
figure and ground into fields of muted colors. While the guest rooms
were furnished with textiles in four different color schemes, they
employed a single carpet pattern, a pointillist array of colored knots
on a neutral background. In 606, a background of light gray wool
is stippled with dots of pink and white. The different hues are
apparent at close range, but when viewed from a distance or at an
angle they blend into a complex shade of warm gray.

Each of the rooms was furnished with window curtains
and bed covers that shared a single pattern of complementary
stripes or geometric shapes. In front of the windows overlooking
Vesterbrogade, dark blue curtains carry light blue stripes that
accent the pleats and continue the vertical rhythm of the window
mullions. When the curtains are drawn, they blend with the valance
and create a band of color that corresponds to the green shade of
the interior walls. The largest room on each floor was provided with

143

a curtain that could be used to screen the beds from the sitting area. In the center of 606, a recessed track in the ceiling supports an open-weave curtain of natural wool. While it is the simplest of the fabrics in the room, this space divider provides the most complex effects of light and texture. At night, backlit by the various lamps, the curtain takes on a gauzy, insubstantial appearance. By day, it appears almost opaque and reveals a rich surface of coarse fibers.

→

View from the top of the spiral stair to the lobby of the Royal Hotel. Panels of gray Plexiglas and a leather-covered railing enclosed the grand stair. A dark green carpet cascaded down the steps, providing an introduction to the parade of fabrics that lined the second floor.

Jacobsen's use of fabric as an architectural device was most apparent on the second floor of the hotel, which housed the bar, the restaurant, and an extended sitting room. While the hotel lobby used contrasting materials and irregular patterns of light to create a dramatic sense of arrival, the second floor combined subdued lighting and coordinated fabrics to cultivate an atmosphere of repose and leisure.

At the top of the suspended promenade that connected the second floor to the lobby, a dark green wool carpet covered in a matrix of lighter squares ran the length of the second floor and established the pattern that would be repeated in the restaurant curtains. Overhead, a ceiling of metal acoustic tiles was painted to match the carpet and perforated by a grid of recessed lights. At the top of the rosewood-paneled walls, the ceiling plane was extended by means of a valance that concealed indirect lighting. These recessed fixtures were used throughout the second floor to create a discreet, luminous border.

Jacobsen arranged the bar, restaurant, and sitting areas on the edges of the second floor, leaving the center to act as a vestibule. The dark surfaces of the floor and ceiling focused attention on the walls, where sheets of glass and stone created veils of reflected light. At opposite ends of the space, the winter garden and the broad glass wall of the restaurant admitted indirect natural light through sets of open-weave curtains. The elevator lobby continued the black marble cladding from below and was furnished with a mirror. Directly across from the elevators, groups of Jacobsen's Series 3300 furniture provided a meeting point and a waiting area for the restaurant. In front of the rosewood panels, a pair of Royal floor lamps served as counterparts to the glossy white columns, and a small case displayed the caviar featured in the restaurant.

A pair of doors in the vestibule walls led to a sitting room overlooking Hammerichsgade. The long narrow space was anchored by the marble-clad piers that supported one end of the tower and subdivided by freestanding walls into seating areas for small groups of guests and visitors. The intimate quality of the narrow room was heightened by the lighting design, which used pools of light to define pockets of space. To one side of the piers, a pair of Swan sofas was lit by a Royal pendant; writing desks nearby were individually lit by Visor wall lamps. To reinforce the contrast between the open vestibule and the private alcoves, Jacobsen covered the floor with a different carpet whose pattern, known as Stav (Staff), resembled a geometric forest.

At the far end of the floor, beyond the stair and obscured by the curtains of the winter garden, lay the secluded Orchid Bar. In spite of its location, the bar served as a condensed version of the hotel's public areas. Pot chairs and a cantilevered sofa were covered in a green fabric that alluded to the vibrant foliage suspended on the walls of the winter garden. Small tables between the chairs were covered in rosewood to continue the dominant material. In one corner, an L-shaped bar was faced in sheets of bronze illuminated from behind, creating an effect like the fixture above the lobby reception desk.

Detail of the stair railing and balustrade. The steel tension rods that supported the delicate steel staircase were painted bright red to articulate their appearance as independent forms.
↓
Second-floor vestibule of the Royal Hotel looking toward the winter garden. The floor was covered in a dark green carpet, and both the ceiling of metal tiles and the wood valances were painted in gray green enamel. The corresponding colors of floor and ceiling drew attention to the walls of wood and glass. Beyond the stair, transparent curtains diffused the light from the winter garden and obscured the hanging light fixtures in the Orchid Bar.

The use of variations on a single form, evident in both the lamps and the furniture, and the combination of recessed and suspended light distinguish the bar as one of Jacobsen's most complex interior spaces. In the restaurant, at the other end of the floor, the themes of the Orchid Bar would, with the addition of hanging fabrics, be expanded into the central public space of the hotel.

Located at the far side of the vestibule, the restaurant had a trio of dining rooms providing 140 seats. In these dining rooms, lighting, textiles, and materials were combined to create a skylit clearing that overlooked both idyllic wonderland (Tivoli Gardens) and industrialized city (the main rail station). Between the vestibule and the main room, a broad wall of glass containing sets of double doors was hung with translucent wool curtains. The hand-woven curtains had a pattern of solid squares that repeated the motif of the carpet and varied in opacity according to the lighting beyond. Private dining rooms on either side of the main room provided an additional twenty seats each. The outer walls of all three dining rooms were hung with solid, white curtains that repeated the pattern of squares, this time in gold embroidery. Bathed in light from the recessed lamps above the valance, the reflections from the gold threads seemed to dissolve the walls in a tapestry of radiant color.

The fabrics and carpets Jacobsen designed for the Royal Hotel were the result of an artistic evolution that began with the representation of nature and evolved into an abstract handling of pattern unique in modern architecture. Though Jacobsen had been designing textiles since 1943, he had used plants as an architectural material from the beginning of his career. In the early years, flowers, living and printed, covered the walls of his interiors. As he refined his artistic vocabulary, Jacobsen replaced the flowers and trees with patterns of line and color. While the contrast between the floral arrangements of the 1940s and the geometric patterns of the SAS House seems abrupt, Jacobsen had spent the intervening decade exploring nuances of pattern and geometry. This change in textile designs evidences his evolution from an illustrator of natural scenes to the creator of his own interior landscapes.

Passage with built-in fluorescent lighting between the winter garden and the sitting rooms. Throughout the second floor of the hotel, built-in lamps provided an even downlight over panels of rosewood and hand-woven curtains.
↓
Elevator lobby. A clock with a face of ground glass was set into a mirror that reflected the seating area along the opposite wall of the vestibule.

→
Writing desks in the sitting room area.
Individual lamps from the Visor Series lit
writing tables with rosewood tops that
matched the paneling. Upholstered armchairs from the Seven Series were covered
in blue green wool.

↘
Sitting room. The piers of the hotel tower
that framed the entry on the floor below
continued through the sitting rooms. In
front of one pier, a pair of special Swan
sofas framed a rosewood table with a
cast-aluminum Shaker base. Overhead, a
brass Royal pendant created an intimate
pool of incandescent light amid the wall-
mounted fluorescent lamps.

↓
Vestibule seating area. Groups of chairs
and sofas from the Series 3300 provided a
convenient gathering point near the
restaurant. In the center, a small glass
case was used to display the local caviar.
Beyond the wall of rosewood panels, the
sitting rooms connected the restaurant
with the Orchid Bar. Jacobsen supplemented the recessed edge lighting with
freestanding floor lamps. These Royal floor
lamps featured shades of open-weave
wool that echoed the forms of the building
columns as well as the translucent
curtains throughout the second floor.

Detail of the Orchid Bar with Pot chairs
and a cantilevered Pot sofa. Both the bar's
hanging fixtures and seating arrangement
illustrate Jacobsen's use of a single ele-
ment to create families of related forms.
The framed prints of antique cars were an
ironic contrast to the modern decor.

Orchid Bar. Behind the winter garden,
this small cocktail lounge was furnished
with Pot chairs and rosewood tables.
In the corner, a bar with backlit bronze
panels was lit by a latticework of Plexiglas panels. Behind the bar, a recessed
niche provided storage for the bottled
goods. The carpet pattern of light green
squares on a dark green field is visible
in the foreground.

Pendant lighting fixture of the Orchid Bar.
Designed in 1959, this simple construction
of smoked Plexiglas sheets was used
throughout the cocktail lounge.

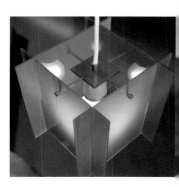

→

View of the Royal Hotel restaurant from the vestibule. The continuous glass wall of the main dining room was cloaked in a curtain of hand-woven wool that repeated the checkerboard motif of the carpet. Along the back wall, an opaque version of the same curtain was embroidered with squares of gold thread that reflected the light from the built-in lamps.

↓

Exterior view of the restaurant skylights. A grid of cylindrical skylights filled the main dining room with daylight. In this night view, the strings of glass bells that were suspended below the glass lens are visible in the center of each opening.

↓↓

Interior detail of the restaurant skylights. Each of the skylights was hung with fifty gray blown-glass bells that tinted the light from above. This repetition of a simple form to create complex effects was typical of Jacobsen's formal economy.

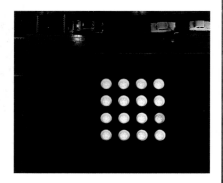

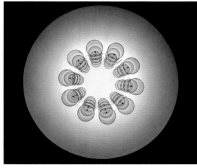

…rivate room of the Royal Hotel restaurant.
…n either side of the main dining room, a
…rivate room served an additional twenty
…eats. Throughout the restaurant, the
…ables were set with flatware and accou-
…ements that Jacobsen had designed
…specially for the hotel.

…oyal Hotel restaurant. The main dining
…oom provided 100 seats beneath a grid of
…bstract chandeliers. During the construc-
…on of the building, Jacobsen removed a
…air of the structural columns to reinforce
…he effect of a clearing in the midst of his
…odular forest.

…etail of the curtain in the Royal Hotel
…estaurant. The curtain along the dining
…oom's glass wall combined Jacobsen's
…ses of interior transparency and geomet-
…c pattern into a single plane of diffused
…ght. Like the room divider in 606, this
…urtain shifted from transparency to opac-
…y depending on the direction of the light
…nd the movement of the viewer.

Crown Imperial wallpaper, 1946. During
their exile in Sweden, Jacobsen and his
wife created a series of designs for wallpaper and fabric that reflected both his
fascination with natural forms and her
background as a textile artist. After re-
turning to Denmark in 1945, Jacobsen
continued his exploration of two-dimensional pattern with designs for a range of
Danish manufacturers.

Jacobsen's *blomstervindue* (flower windows), his abstract versions of the traditional English bay window, were usually located on a southern corner and projected beyond the faces of the building. By juxtaposing views of the surroundings with living plants, these miniature winter gardens created dramatic impressions of continuous space and seasonal contrast. In the public buildings that followed his early houses, Jacobsen used layers of leaves and flowers to draw a connection between modern architecture and the natural world. At the Bellevue restaurant, completed in 1937 as part of a seaside leisure complex at Klampenborg, the walls of the summer dining room were lined with bamboo staves that supported creeping vines and created the impression of a whitewashed grotto. In front of walls of translucent glass, the staves were anchored in deep planters that contained flowering plants and small trees. Five years later, Jacobsen covered the walls of the civil wedding room at Søllerød Town Hall with a floral wallpaper that created an atmosphere of perennial springtime. While there is no record that Jacobsen designed the pattern himself, this use of printed flowers was a first step toward the textiles that would blend his passion for nature with his penchant for abstract form.

Jacobsen's lifelong preoccupation with the plant kingdom was rooted in his early experiences in watercolor painting. As an indifferent student at boarding school, Jacobsen discovered his artistic talents when a sympathetic teacher provided him with a box of watercolors. In his adolescence, he earned pocket money by selling his paintings of plants and landscapes to his instructors and fellow students. During World War II, painting served as both a personal refuge and a critical step in his artistic development. Produced under the tragic circumstances of wartime, Jacobsen's textiles of the 1940s are the crucial link between his interior gardens of the 1930s and the abstract patterns and modular buildings of his later years.

Germany invaded Denmark in early 1940. For the next three years, most of Denmark's estimated 8,000 Jewish citizens were sheltered by friends and neighbors, and the Germans focused their attention on Denmark's agricultural output. In the summer of 1943, however, the German government decreed that Danish Jews would be deported to the concentration camps in the east. Following advance warning from the Nazi functionary who governed the country, the majority of the Jewish population was spirited to neutral Sweden in rowboats and fishing vessels. On the night of 30 September 1943, Jacobsen, his second wife, Jonna, and their friends Mr. and Mrs. Poul Henningsen took flight in a rowboat across the sound. The Jacobsens made their way to Stockholm, where Alvar Aalto helped them to find an apartment and where Jacobsen was given a position at the Swedish national building cooperative.

Jonna Jacobsen had been trained as a textile printer; before their flight, the Jacobsens had been in contact with Nordiske Kompaniet, the leading department store in Stockholm, regarding a line of fabrics and wallpapers. Leveraging their professional contacts, Jacobsen and his wife arranged to produce designs that would be manufactured at the NK textile workshop run by Astrid Sampe

↑

Bellevue theater and restaurant, Klampen-borg, 1935–37. In the 1930s, Jacobsen filled his buildings with interior plantings that provided texture and color to his austere surfaces.

↗

Wedding reception room in Søllerød Town Hall, Søllerød, 1939–42. The walls of the reception room were covered in a two-dimensional pattern of local flowers. While Jacobsen did not design this wall-paper, the corollation between its painted bouquets and the creeping vines of his earlier work are obvious.

↓

Exhibition of decorative arts, Nordiske Kompaniet department store, Stockholm, 1944. The Jacobsens's wartime textiles were not only commercially successful: a two-week exhibition displayed the fabrics as works of applied art, and the Swedish National Museum purchased a set for its permanent collection. In the

foreground, a couple examines the design for Höstlöv, one of the fifteen patterns available in forty-five colorways

←

Höstlöv, printed curtain fabric, 1943–44. Clusters of falling sycamore and beech leaves in shades of brown and orange coalesce on the surface of the fabric, while seedpods fade into the white back-ground and create an impression of depth. The naturalistic patterns that Jacobsen designed during the 1940s provided a formative training in the composition of color and contour.

and sold at the department store. Working out of their small, government-supplied apartment, the Jacobsens collaborated on a series of patterns for printed fabrics and wallpaper, with Arne producing tempera paintings that his wife would translate into serigraph screens. In 1944, the fabrics were exhibited at the NK store in Stockholm, where they were displayed like tapestries. Following the exhibition, a set of fabrics was acquired by the Swedish National Museum. These early representations of nature were both the beginning of Jacobsen's career as a textile artist and the first step in his evolution toward a language of abstract pattern.

The floral designs for NK were a commercial as well as a critical success, and Jacobsen continued to create designs for Swedish manufacturers until as late as 1948, when Strüwing photographed a group of Jacobsen's most recent designs, including a pattern called Tulips. While the wartime prints had depicted scenes of nature taken from meadows and forests, Tulips was a floating composition that layered vibrant and muted colors to dissolve conventions of depth and pictorial illusion. Between the solid blossoms, striped petals shot through with the background colors of green and white suggest a reversal of figure and ground. Crown Imperial, a wallpaper design dating from the same period, moved further toward an abstract composition. Clusters of plants were dissolved by drooping tulips that appear to recede into the white background, creating visual holes in the picture plane, while sprays of green leaves burst forward and float along the surface.

In the early 1950s, Jacobsen began to flatten the flowers into two-dimensional shapes and to experiment with color. A painting for a printed fabric of blossoms from 1952 displays Jacobsen's use of natural form as an armature for abstract compositions. While the bright surfaces of the leaves recede into a blue background of equal value, veins and shadowed areas are pushed to the surface, leaving an irregular arrangement of floating forms and lines. An undated painting of flowers that resemble poppies suggests the visual equivalent of musical scales, as Jacobsen explores effects of color and value in burnt earth tones and the blues and greens that would anchor his final palette.

Within a few years, Jacobsen's flowers had dissolved into patterns of color and geometry, and he began to produce designs for a range of Danish manufacturers, including August Millech, Grautex, and C. Olesen. Pure geometry had made a subtle appearance in his printed fabrics as early as 1951 with Collier, a pattern of light stars on a dark background. In fact, the stars were the remnants of a background obscured by blocks of overlapping circles that alternated with squares of solid color. Relying on contrasts of light and dark and ambiguity between foreground and background to imply a sense of depth, Collier was one of the most complex of Jacobsen's printed fabrics, and it provided a model for the gridded curtains that lined the restaurant of the Royal Hotel. Tasco, a printed curtain from 1956, abandoned any overt reference to nature to create floating rectangles that used negative space to produce an animated field of irregular bars.

→
Gouache sketch for Blomster, 1952.
↓
Tulips, printed cotton fabric, 1948. Jacobsen continued his work in textile designs
even as his architecture practice flour-
ished at the end of the 1940s. This design
signaled a looser, more abstract approach,
as the picture plan is eroded by advancing
and receding bursts of color.

Jacobsen used flowers to explore compositions of complementary colors and contrasting shapes. As these designs became
ever more abstract, the flowers were
transformed into geometric shapes and
the colors veered toward monochromes.

→
Gouache sketch for curtain fabric,
c. 1954.
↘
Untitled color study, c. 1952.
↘ ↘
Pencil study for Linier, 1957.
↓
Watercolor study, c. 1955.

This survey of curtain fabrics summarizes Jacobsen's synthesis of nature and geometry. In the decade between his return from Sweden and the design of the SAS House, Jacobsen's patterns moved from illustration to composition. The relationship between the textiles and the contemporary buildings underscores the role of textile design as Jacobsen's bridge between natural and artificial landscapes.

←

Ditch Flowers, printed cotton fabric, 1944.

↙

Collier, printed cotton fabric, 1951.

↓

Trapeze, printed cotton fabric, 1949.

↓
Tasco, printed cotton fabric, 1957.
↘
Cirkul, printed cotton fabric, c. 1957.

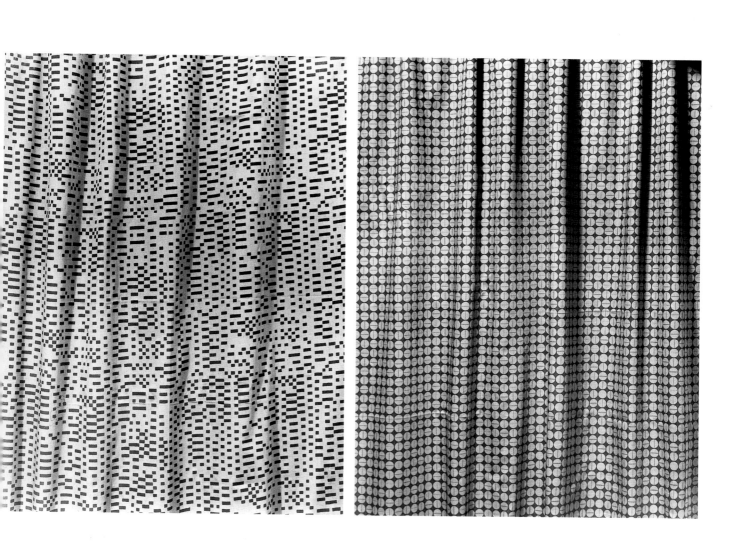

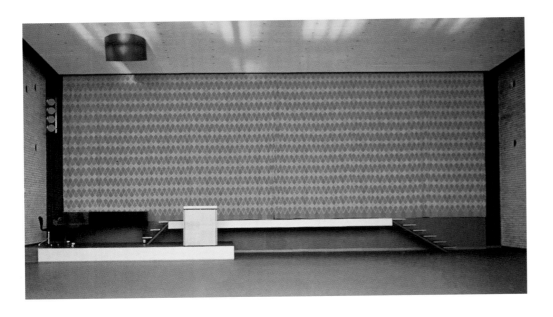

Auditorium with stage curtain, Munkegård School, Gentofte, 1948–57. The vivid backdrop was both a means of focusing attention on the stage and a corollary to the paving designs of the individual courtyards.

Munkegård School auditorium with transparent curtain. Along the north wall of the auditorium, a transparent mesh repeated the structure of the stage curtain in a monochromatic reversal of figure and ground. The contrasting veils, united by a single pattern, served as the model for the curtains of the restaurant in the Royal Hotel.

Jacobsen continued to design patterns as an artistic outlet even as his practice expanded and he achieved international recognition. In 1957, the Copenhagen department store Magasin du Nord held an open, anonymous competition for new designs for curtains and carpets. An article in *Dansk Kunsthaandvaerk* later in the year reported that Jacobsen had been awarded first prize for Linier, a woven fabric of alternating lines, and third prize for Ringe, a carpet pattern of rings that were woven in complementary colors. In spite of this growing emphasis on geometry, nature remained the foundation of Jacobsen's visual vocabulary. Evidence of his persistent naturalism is preserved at the library of the Royal Academy, where the original drawing for Linier shares a folder with a photostat of a man standing behind a waterfall. The streams of falling water create an irregular field of light and shadow; its resemblence to Linier points to Jacobsen's gift for transforming nature into his own world of forms.

The most vibrant of Jacobsen's geometric textiles was the stage curtain he designed in 1955 for the assembly hall of the Munkegård School. The pattern combined the chromatic palette of Tulips with the delicate linework of Arabic ornament in a shimmering web of color, fifteen meters wide and 4.25 meters high. The curtain was hand-woven in the workshop of Kirsten and John Becker, the leading textile artisans of the time. The Beckers used coarse flax, dyed a deep scarlet, as the base for six different shades of wool yarn that would create a vivid pattern of alternating squares and polygons separated by a net of white lines. The relationship between Jacobsen's textile designs and his modular glass buildings of the same period was made explicit in the other curtain he designed for the assembly hall. A broad wall of glass at the north end of the hall was covered with a translucent version of the stage curtain, repeating its visual structure in a mesh of black lines. The opposition between color and line and the layering of the delicate linework over the expanse of glass present a woven equivalent to the curtain walls at Rødovre Town Hall and the SAS House. Five years later, Jacobsen and the Beckers collaborated again on the pair of curtains that lined the Royal Hotel restaurant in alternating patterns of reflected and transmitted light.

In the designs that followed the Munkegård curtains, Jacobsen adopted an increasingly muted palette, with vivid contrasts replaced by variations in texture. A drawing for the living room of the Hansaviertel courtyard house, constructed in Berlin for the 1957 building exhibition, is collaged with swatches of fabric that signal a return to the colors of the garden. Both the gouache study and the printed design for a curtain called Cirkul play upon optical effects of shading and density to create a pattern that dissolves into the background. Following the SAS House, Jacobsen concentrated on overall ensembles of color and material. The results can be seen in a watercolor from the competition scheme for the Industri Hus (Industry House), an office building that was projected on the west edge of the Radhuspladsen in 1964.

Jacobsen's designs for wallpaper, fabrics, and carpeting might be considered a diversion. Rather than a sideline, however,

↑
Watercolor of typical office interior,
Industry House, Copenhagen, 1964
(competition entry). The abstraction of
Jacobsen's later buildings was matched
by a palette of colors and finishes
that served as the final evidence of his
horticultural model.
→
Watercolor of the Industry House plaza
facing the town hall. In spite of the futur-
istic forms of this unbuilt office building,
Jacobsen's lifelong romanticism is evident
in the lush plantings and reflecting basins.

→
Drawing of living room with fabric swatches,
Hansaviertel courtyard houses, Berlin,
1955–57. After 1955, Jacobsen's textiles
became increasingly muted as he relied
upon solid color and subtle texture to
produce naturalistic effects. This study for
the interior of a single-family house used
rough wool curtains to relate the walls to
furniture and hint at the richness of the
interior garden beyond.

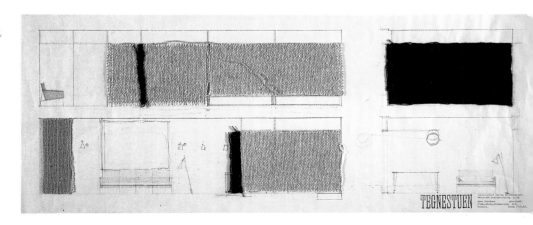

hese exercises in two-dimensional composition were of central importance to his architectural development. The floral patterns of he mid-1940s were an opportunity for Jacobsen to focus on attern and color and provided the training ground for his movement toward abstract form. Over the fifteen years that elapsed between Jacobsen's return from exile and the completion of the SAS building, textile design assumed a central role in his artistic production. Mirroring their evolution from wartime necessity to creative outlet, the designs reflected his developing command of abstraction to create surfaces that offered both restrained color and subtle visual effects. In contrast to the picturesque depictions of the countryside that he painted while in Sweden, the fabrics of the 1950s rendered fields of lines and shapes in a drastically reduced palette of blues and greens. This emphasis on repetitive figures paralleled the development of Jacobsen's architecture that began in 1948 with the standard classrooms of the Munkegård School and culminated in the curtain wall of the SAS House.

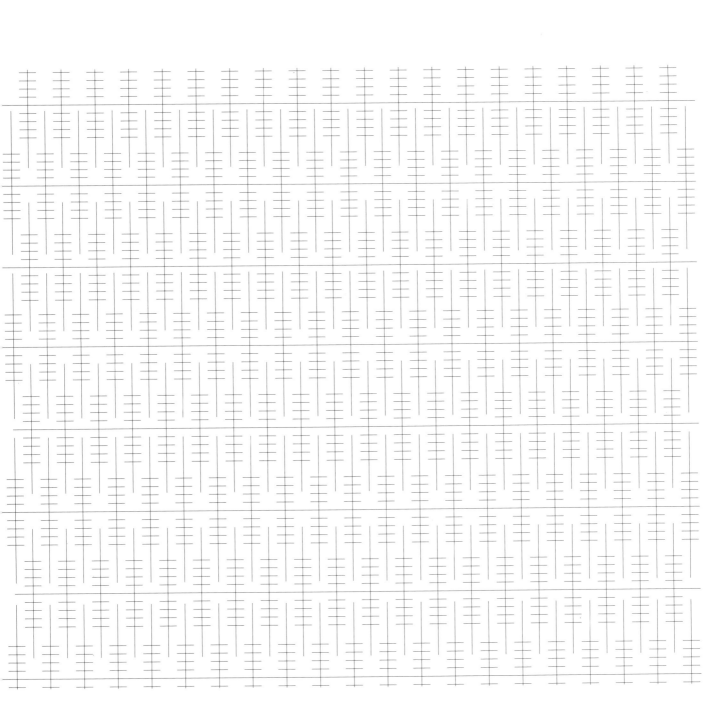

→
Room 606, Royal Hotel, SAS House, Copenhagen, 1955-60. Bedside tables with a single drawer are cantilevered from the built-in paneling. The tables, supported by steel brackets that fit into the reveals between the panels, can be mounted at two heights.

he woodwork that lines Room 606 serves as both paneling and
able, blurring the distinction between building and furnishings. On
he interior walls, thin slots—reveals—divide the wenge veneer into
nodular units. To one side of the door leading to the vestibule, steel
rackets mounted in the reveals project into the room and support
string of wood boxes at desk height. Pairs of similar boxes at the
ar end of the room are hung at a lower level to serve as night-
tands for the twin beds. These boxes' width corresponds to the
ystem of panels; they are covered in matching wood, while their
ops are faced with blue plastic laminate that matches the
windowsill. The paneling continues along the room's outer wall in
continuous surface that corresponds to the painted blue valance
bove the windows.

The joints between the panels, set on a sixty-centimeter
nodule, establish a vertical rhythm that is echoed by the window
mullions. The wood below the window is continuous in order to con-
eal the difference in widths between the one-meter windows and
he fifty-centimeter paneling. Beyond this visual relationship
etween exterior (mullions) and interior (panels), the variation of
he panel's wood grain provides a small-scale rendition of the con-
rast between modular order and natural variation that is the defin-
ng feature of the SAS House's exterior. The contrast of geometric
rder and the natural variation in wood grain also provides a
rivate analogue to the urban tapestry of the exterior glazing.

With its intersection of traditional craft and modern mate-
ials, natural pattern and geometric order, Jacobsen's system of
aneling and wall-hung boxes must be considered one of the rep-
esentative designs of his work. Throughout his career, he sought
o create type-forms, elementary objects that could be adapted to
variety of locations. The Visor lamps and Seven series of chairs
re two of the most notable examples. While the woodwork in Room

↑
Room 606. Jacobsen designed the wall-hung boxes to perform a range of functions. In the sitting area, units with two drawers alternate with dressing tables. A hinged top with a mirror and integral light provides a makeup table with interior storage.

→
Sketch for a dressing table, 1958. Jacobsen had originally imagined that the tables would be topped with wenge and faced with plastic laminate. In the final design, this idea was reversed as he extended the laminate to protect the writing surface and covered the fronts of the units with wenge. The resulting wall-hung boxes act as extensions of the paneling and reinforce the role of the woodwork as an interior lining.

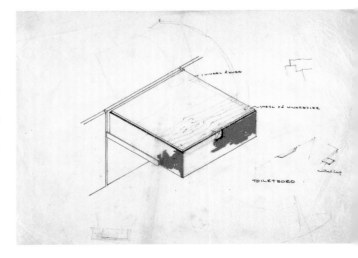

606 extends Jacobsen's motif of suspended pattern at the scale of the room, the uniform width of the panels and tables allow the furnishings to be rearranged or exchanged with any of the other rooms.

As he worked across the boundaries between architecture and the applied arts, Jacobsen used geometric pattern to unite different surfaces and objects into an integrated environment. As a result, the exterior curtain wall, the interiors of the public areas and the individual hotel rooms were experienced as a continuous progression of gridded planes that were enriched by nuances of natural variation. The system of panels and cantilevered tables was the most intricate of Jacobsen's gridded structures and it provided the underlying order for the layout of the tower floors.

Exhibition layout, Musée des Arts Décoratifs, Paris, 1958. Jacobsen planned the
public introduction of the SAS House with
the same care with which he designed the
furnishings. His sketch for the installation
details the precise location and lighting
for the woodwork, furniture, and textiles.

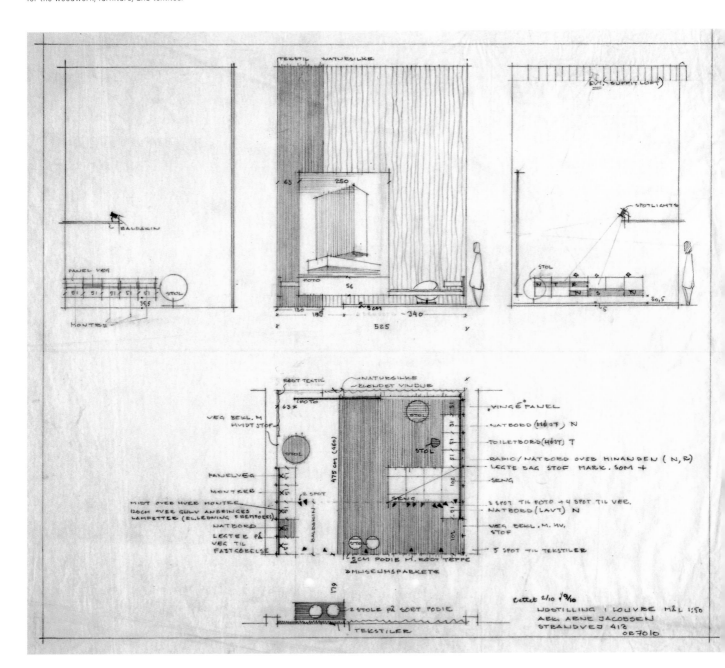

Jacobsen's greatest challenge in designing the SAS House was providing the hotel with a range of rooms, which varied in size and location, with a single system of furnishings and materials. The building was designed on a square grid, 4.8 meters on a side, that was based on the spacing of the columns in the structure along Hammerichsgade. Subdivisions of this grid, 240, 120, and 60 centimeters, were used to determine the width of the elements and surfaces in the building, from the stone paving of the lobby floor to the mullion spacing of the curtain wall. This modular system allowed precise alignments between different materials and insured an organic harmony between the whole and the parts. The hotel rooms reflected this system, integrating the module of the curtain wall. To accomplish this, Jacobsen invented a system of woodwork that would be used throughout the 275 rooms to provide a uniform system of flexible, built-in furnishings. The result was a virtual forest of wenge veneer, cut into fifty-centimeter panels and suspended above the rooftops of Copenhagen.

The ascent into the tower of suspended woodwork began in the elevator lobbies of the lower floors. Paneled in oak and illuminated by translucent Plexiglas ceilings, the landings provided a dramatic transition from the dramatic lighting of the public floors to the sunlit rooms of the tower. The elevators' walls of wenge paneling divided by stainless steel bars provided the transition. The third floor, poised between tower and base, contained machinery rooms and the office of the building manager behind floor-to-ceiling windows recessed to articulate the division between tower and base. The floor above housed the offices of the hotel management as well as an employee canteen and a pair of dormitories providing accommodations for the hotel staff.

The hotel rooms occupied the fifth through twenty-second floors of the building. The tower's typical floors each contained sixteen rooms of various sizes. To avoid the anonymity of an unbroken hallway and to provide a subtle transition between the corridor and the individual rooms, Jacobsen recessed the doors in subtle niches, lit from above. A shallow alcove opposite the elevators was furnished with a Pot chair, creating a focal point for the corridor and a meeting place for hotel guests.

Each of the guest rooms was entered through a vestibule that included closets and the entrance to the bathroom. This separation between bed and bath allowed greater privacy and heightened the effect of domesticity that Jacobsen cultivated throughout the building. The four corners of each floor were occupied by double rooms with bathrooms along the ends of the tower that provided unparalled views over the city. Between the corner rooms, the floor was divided into single and double rooms that varied from ten to twenty square meters. Most of these rooms contained an interior double door that permitted the rooms to be occupied en suite, increasing the range of possible accomodations. In the middle of each floor, a special double room (of which 606 is an example) was provided with an expanded vestibule and an additional toilet. The four corners of each floor were occupied by double rooms (fifteen square meters) with bathrooms

along the end walls; the continuous windows afforded guests unparalleled views while bathing. Two rows of single (ten to twelve square meters) and double (eighteen to twenty square meters) rooms were entered through vestibules that separated the bathrooms and closets from the sleeping rooms. Each floor also contained a special double room (thirty square meters) opposite the elevators with a larger vestibule and an additional toilet.

Floors twenty and twenty-one were made up of suites, all with additional sitting areas and furnished with a variety of special cabinets and color schemes. The number of suites on the twenty-first floor was reduced to accommodate a pair of special areas. The entire west end of the floor was devoted to the director's apartment and the on-site residence for the hotel chef and his family, who undoubtedly found the lack of a kitchen a small sacrifice for the seven rooms and two baths with a view west to the edge of the city. A spiral stair just outside the director's door led to the twenty-second floor where, amid air-handling equipment and a 10,000-gallon reservoir for the sprinkler system, Jacobsen located a spa featuring a four-room sauna, massage rooms, and ultraviolet tanning equipment. At the east end of the floor was the Panorama Room, a lounge with views over the city and harbor, the sound, and beyond to Sweden. Paneled in Douglas fir and furnished with Swan chairs and bronze-plated versions of the AJ Royal pendant lamp, the room formed a radiant contrast to the subdued palette of greens and blues in the guest rooms.

From the beginning of the project, Jacobsen had imagined a system of wall-mounted furniture that would maximize the open space within the guest rooms and unite the beds, luggage racks, and tables in a single system of wall-mounted units. Realizing that a modular system would allow the rooms to be easily rearranged, he settled on a unit of fifty centimeters, one-half the width of a standard bed. The earliest sketches of guest rooms depict tables and shelving units that are cantilevered from the paneling at various heights. As the design developed, Jacobsen standardized the units into a simple box of fifty by fifty by fifteen centimeters. The boxes were mounted at two different heights and covered in blue plastic laminate, while their tops were wenge veneer. While this scheme coordinated the boxes with the window valance, Jacobsen ultimately inverted the materials to emphasize the boxes as an extension of the paneling. With this substitution Jacobsen united modular systems of furnishing and paneling into a series of vertical surfaces that would tie the interior of the room to the curtain wall.

In Jacobsen's most integrated works, a handful of basic forms were elaborated in a wide range of materials to create an organic sense of harmony between the whole and its parts. Building, furnishings, and textiles were treated as exercises in modular construction, in which a basic unit is repeated to produce variations on a form. The SAS House employed this principle at both the structural and the cellular scales. At the small end of this scale, the uniform size of the boxes allowed combinations of variable length to be installed in any of the guest rooms. The steel brackets that held the boxes could be inserted into any of the identical corresponding gaps between

Views of the elevator lobby of the Royal Hotel. At the base of the tower, the elevator lobby used contrasting woods to reinforce the effect of movable cabins. The walls of the vestibule were paneled in oak that reflected the warm white light from the fluorescent lamps overhead. The elevator doors and cabins were paneled in wenge, with stainless steel frames and divider strips that presaged the modular paneling in the guest rooms.

Seating alcove. On each floor, a deeper niche was located opposite the elevators. These seating alcoves were decorated with a work of art and furnished with a Pot chair in dark brown leather.

Typical corridor. The corridors were designed to prevent an impression of excessive length. The low ceiling was painted white, and the gray green doors to the guest rooms were placed in individual niches with overhead lighting.

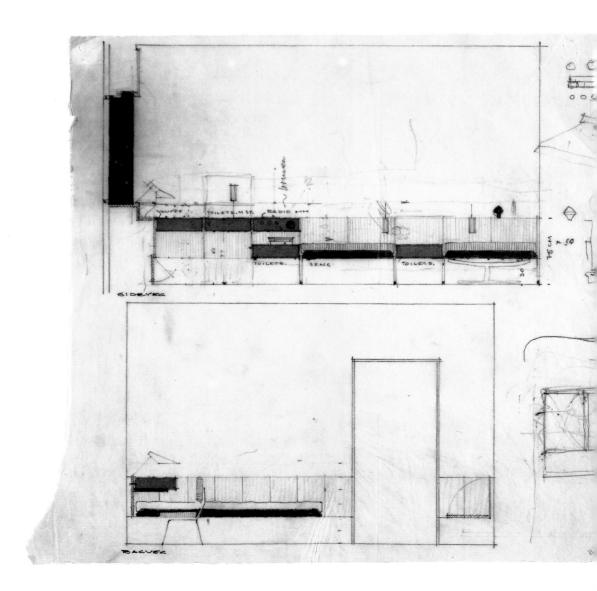

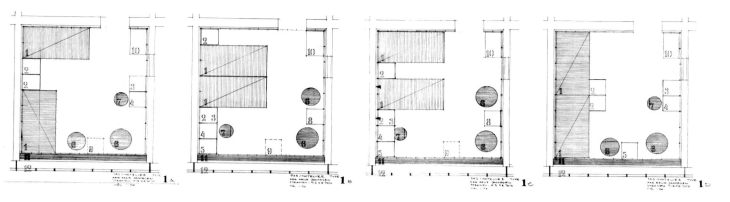

↑

Diagrams of a double room, 1960. The system of built-in paneling and cantilevered tables allowed the furnishings to be rearranged according to the needs of the guests. Diagrams exploring the possible configurations illustrate the flexibility that was inherent in Jacobsen's modular system.

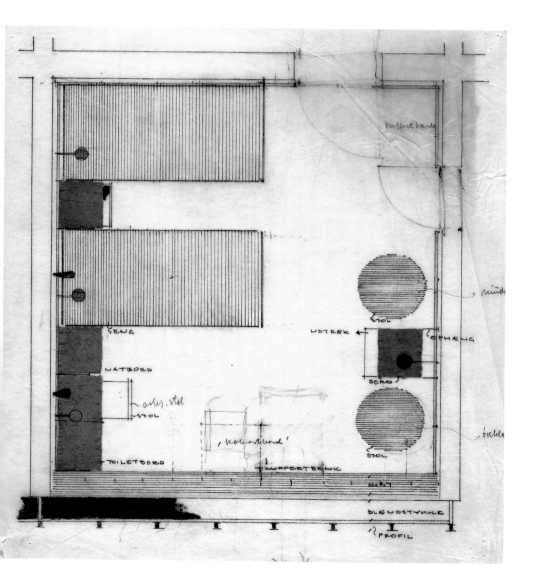

←←

Plan and interior elevations of a typical double room, 1958. Design drawings illustrate Jacobsen's attempts to integrate all of the furnishings into a series of wall-hung units. The interior elevations depict a stacked arrangement of tables, a cantilevered luggage rack, and a folding shelf. The only lighting fixture is a sliding lamp along the windowsill.

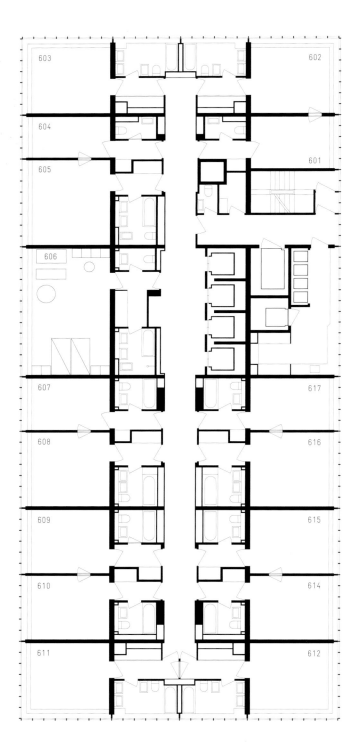

↑

Typical hotel rooms. Across a range of
sizes and configurations, all 275 rooms
of the Royal Hotel were outfitted with
Jacobsen's novel system of paneling and
storage.

↙

Plan of a typical floor, Royal Hotel, 1:200.
The guest rooms were organized around a
double-loaded corridor with bands of
rooms along the north and south faces of
the tower. Each bedroom had a vestibule
containing a closet and the door to the
bathroom. Connecting doors allowed adjacent rooms to be joined. In the corner
rooms, the bathrooms were placed along
the exterior wall, providing spectacular
views over Copenhagen.

↓

Chest of drawers and writing table, 1960.
The suites on the nineteenth floor provided
an opportunity for special furnishings that
offered variations on the wall-hung boxes
and corresponded to the proportions of the
paneling.

→
Detail of wall-hung box. Each room was furnished with a unit that contained a volume knob and preset buttons for the radio system that was wired to built-in speakers in the ceiling. On the right side of the unit, a trio of buttons, red, green, and white, activated a light in the corridor that indicated the desired degree of privacy.

↓
Royal system. The fifty-centimeter-wide wall-hung boxes corresponded in width to the wood panels, which were divided by one-centimeter-wide vertical reveals. Along the top of the paneling, a continuous horizontal reveal was outfitted with reading lamps that could slide along the walls.

↑
Panorama Room, view over Copenhagen looking east to the Øresund.
→
Panorama Room. On the twenty-first
floor of the Royal Hotel, the use of
wood paneling to frame the landscape was expanded to fill the width
of the tower. The wenge was replaced by Douglas fir, and the
lighter wood was complemented by
the bronze metalwork of the seating
and light fixtures.

the panels. Individual boxes could serve a wide range of functions; some were outfitted with drawers of various sizes, while others contained electrical apparatuses including radio equipment,
buttons for summoning hotel staff, and controls for the lights in the corridor that indicated whether
the room was available for housekeeping. The most elaborate variation was the dressing table,
which had a hinged top that opened to reveal a mirror and a pressure-sensitive switch that activated a light when opened. In the suites on the upper floors, where space limitations were not a
concern, Jacobsen created freestanding variations of the boxes, including writing desks and
chests of drawers.

Jacobsen's built-in woodwork was the fundamental feature of the hotel guest rooms, and
it joined his primary artistic themes in a virtuoso combination of utility and beauty. The elegant
rhythm of the vertical panels and their alignment with the sill of the window wall set into motion
the experience of an interior landscape. The creation of a single unit that could be repositioned
from wall to wall, room to room, or floor to floor encapsulated his aesthetic functionalism in a
single deft stroke. The use of richly patterned hardwood, with natural variations that are subor-
dinated to a modular system, is a vivid example of his pursuit of an abstract equivalent of the
natural world.

↓
Teller windows, Landmandsbanken,
St. Stefan's branch, Copenhagen, 1936.
Fabricated with Jacobsen's characteristic
attention to utility and visual delight, a
continuous brass light fixture, embellished
by painted script, lit delicate panels of
wood and glass.

Jacobsen's remarkable system of wood paneling and demountable wall-hung bureaus that filled the 275 guest rooms of the hotel had antecedents in the built-in cabinetry and wood constructions he had designed over the previous thirty years. While the curved wooden walls and lavish veneers at Aarhus Town Hall reflected the influence of Erik Gunnar Asplund, its built-in storage systems were profoundly influenced by the conservative empiricism of Professor Kaare Klint.

In 1924, Klint was appointed the first professor of furniture design at the Royal Academy, where he developed a novel curriculum that would influence Danish furniture design and construction for the rest of the century. Klint's methods, evident in both his teaching and his own canonical furniture, combined a thorough study of historical precedents, seeking dimensional and proportional constants, with patient research into the objects of daily life. A project for a sideboard would commence with the detailed study and measurement of cutlery, china, and glassware in an effort to identify its most compact form possible. In contrast to the Bauhaus, which rejected historical models and traditional materials, Klint's combination of anthropological study and functionalist research imbued his students with a methodology that could be applied to a range of articles, regardless of form or means of production. The importance of these lessons for Jacobsen's development cannot be overestimated. Their initial fruition came in a trio of small commercial projects designed between 1935 and 1948.

In 1935, as the Bellevue theater and restaurant were nearing completion, Jacobsen was commissioned to design branch offices of the Landmandsbanken for three locations in the center of Copenhagen. While no images of the first branch at Vesterbro Torv survive, photographs of the other two offices record the use of built-in furnishings and careful detailing to produce an atmosphere of domestic comfort within a commercial setting. To create a common identity between the different locations, Jacobsen focused his attention on the furnishings for both bank staff and customers. At both branches, he created built-in writing desks that faced the street through broad sheets of glass. Continuous brass lighting fixtures above these desks illuminated the writing surface and various paperwork.

Beyond the customer waiting areas, elaborately detailed tellers' counters reflected the different structures of the existing buildings. At the St. Stefan branch at 160 Nørrebrogade, the twin piers of the building were used to frame the counters, which were veneered in sycamore and lit by a continuous brass trough that repeated the fixture of the writing desk (and foreshadowed the fixture of the SAS travel agency). At the St. Jørgen branch at 37 Vester Farimagsgade, a single column provided an anchor for an undulating counter of sycamore veneer, subdivided by etched glass screens that repeated the pattern of the linoleum floor.

In 1948, Jacobsen was asked to design the new offices of L. Paulsen A/S, a coffee importer. The director of Paulsen, Rüthwen Jürgensen, was an old friend. The firm had leased a floor of a grand neoclassical building at 19 Frederiksgade, on a formal square over-

↑
Exterior of the Landmandsbanken,
St. Stefan's branch. Jacobsen's work for
the bank consisted of remodeling the
commercial space in a series of older
buildings. All three of the remodeled
branches featured a large display window
and neon signage that announced the contemporary identity of the institution.

↙
Interior of the St. Stefan's branch. Within
the shells of the each building, Jacobsen
used built-in seating, wood paneling, and
a distinctive floor of inset linoleum to create a unique interior. At the St. Stefan's
branch, sycamore veneers and warm
leather upholstery produced a sense of
comfortable luxury.

↙ ↙
Lobby of the St. Jørgen's branch, Copenhagen. The lobby was furnished with
Jacobsen's own furniture, including the
Bellevue chair along the customer desk
and a set of upholstered chairs that fore-
shadow the voluptuous shells of the Egg
and the Swan. The curving service counter
and the window were paneled in teak,
and the etched glass teller screens repeated the floor pattern.

↓
Customer desk in the St. Jørgen's branch.
Below the picture window, a built-in desk
with a glass top provided the customers
with an area for filling out paperwork.
Beneath the glass top, banknotes and
other financial documents were treated as
functional decoration.

ooking Frederikskirken, the neo-baroque church that dominates Copenhagen's Amalienborg district. The glass-and-wood interiors Jacobsen created within the loadbearing shell of the old building were essentially large-scale cabinets. To make the most of available light in the narrow, deep floor, the offices were subdivided by partitions of glass outfitted with hanging blinds. Jacobsen provided a test kitchen, sample room, and reception room with a range of built-in furnishings and custom fittings, including a very elegant spittoon. These rooms were inserted into the neoclassical shell like large pieces of cabinetry.

The Paulsen commission was modest, but it allowed Jacobsen to explore three critical strategies that would culminate in the ground floor of the SAS House: the use of transparent partitions would, along with his adoption of the international vernacular of the frame and curtain wall, be extended to encompass the building itself; built-in fittings, which he created for a number of commercial buildings in the 1930s, were realized at a new level of craftsmanship and eventually led to the furnishings of the Royal Hotel guest rooms; finally, while Jacobsen had always practiced the art of display and the arrangement of precious objects—in his home and his clients'—the Paulsen offices were a training ground and an insular prototype for the extravagant window displays that would define the street fronts of the SAS House.

The definitive transformation from an inserted object or applied panel to the substance of a building occurred at the Munkegård School. There, below a continuous slot vent in the windowless brick north wall of the science, art, craft, music, and cooking building, Jacobsen created a thickened wall that was hollowed out to provide storage and display for tools, instruments, and so on, appropriate to each classroom. The Munkegård cabinet-wall is a modular system, its paneling widths conforming to the 140-centimeter module of the curtain wall that faces south. In contrast to earlier examples such as at the Stelling Building, where built-in cabinetry was inserted into a space, the storage wall at Munkegård was integrated into the building itself. It contained ventilation equipment and served to define the classrooms, becoming the effective interplay between interior and exterior, room and envelope.

At the 1961 Wandel House, the cabinetry and woodwork Jacobsen used to integrate building and furniture, structure and interior, was expanded to become the interior architecture. This, Jacobsen's final freestanding house, served as a return to his origins and highlighted both his conceptual consistency and his formal evolution. On a small, flat parcel in Ordrup subdivided from the land containing his 1934 house for Helge Wandel, Jacobsen was commissioned to design a new house for Wandel's widow, Gerte. Like the first Wandel House, the new house would be a brick building that engaged the landscape with gardens and large expanses of glass. But its radically different approach to form and garden illustrated the completeness of Jacobsen's personal language.

The Wandel House was designed around a series of cabinets, organized along a central corridor and enclosed by parallel walls of brick that framed carefully composed episodes of nature.

→

Main office area, L. Paulsen A/S offices, Copenhagen, 1946. The main area was divided by panels of glass that could be screened for privacy. At either end of the open office, built-in shelves of mahogany provided storage for ledgers. Custom desks combined mahogany frames with cedar panels.

↙

Testing rooms. The offices included a suite of rooms devoted to blending, sampling, and testing coffee. The blending table was set into the window well and framed by aromatic cedar panels and matching wood blinds.
↓

Testing kitchen. Beyond the blending room the kitchen was furnished with a counter of Cuban mahogany used for the display and preparation of coffee. The turned legs of the counter repeated the module of the woven reed panels that lined the walls.
↓ ↓

Detail of the sorting table.

Hall of the Stelling House, Copenhagen, 1934–37. The street-level hall, outfitted with teak counters and shelving, was devoted to paint and displayed thousands of different hues. Adjustable counter lamps and two kinds of hanging lamps provided a mix of task and ambient light. The wall of shelves and the curving wood counter formed an interior lining that mirrored the curve of the street wall.

↓

Display window of the Stelling House. The windows of the retail store were filled with spectacular arrangements of pigments and artist's equipment. The wall-mounted lamps and freestanding fixtures once again exemplify Jacobsen's goal of providing his clients with an integrated architectural solution.

...tchen of the Munkegård School, Gentofte,
...948–57. While the standard classrooms
...ere multi-use spaces with lightweight
...rniture, the two-story building along the
...ack of the school was filled with special-
...ed facilities and classrooms. The school
...tchens were planned by Jacobsen and
...quipped with wooden storage units that
...tegrated ovens, counters, and drawers
...to a single freestanding island.

...oodworking classrooms in the
...unkegård School. The walls were covered
...ith panels of book-matched birch veneer
...nd incorporated storage units with slid-
...g tambour doors. Above the storage
...nits, hinged panels provided access to
...e ventilation duct that extended along
...e back of the building. The entire setting
...rovided an object lesson in the rewards
... precise craftsmanship.

↑
Exterior, Gerte Wandel House, Gentofte,
1960–61. The insular character of
Jacobsen's last house was announced by
the massive brick wall that contained the
garage door and the windows to the guest
bedrooms. In the background, a cleft
between the walls led to the entry.

Corridor of the Wandel House. To one side
of the corridor, doors and storage closets
were joined in a wall of painted wood that
contrasted with the rough brick surface
opposite. The corridor was paved with
brick and had a wood ceiling, providing
both spatial and material continuity along
the length of the house.

Detail of the corridor. The wooden wall
that lined the corridor continued beyond
the interior doors, reinforcing the effect of
a continuous wooden box inserted between
the brick walls. In the background, the
patio served as an interior garden.

View of the library from the living room.
The physical and emotional center of
the house was a wall of shelving with an
integral fireplace.

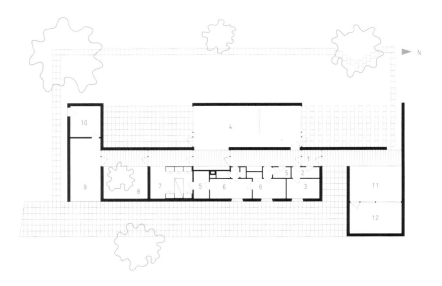

← Plan, Wandel House, 1:400. The house consisted of solid brick walls, which contained a small courtyard and framed the views of the site. The interior of the house was organized around a corridor that extended the length of the building and was subdivided by sets of glass doors and windows.

1 Vestibule
2 Pantry
3 Kitchen
4 Living/dining room
5 Bathroom
6 Guest bedrooms
7 Master bedroom
8 Courtyard
9 Garage
10 Boiler room
11 Drying court
12 Laundry room

↓ Corridor and bedroom. The wood service wall continued into the owner's bedroom, providing a series of closets with integrated louvers for ventilation.

A thick wall formed an interior lining that repeated the building module and defined the layer of private rooms beyond the corridor. Glass walls at either end of a living/dining area framed views of small gardens. At the center of the house, a library and fireplace tied corridor to living room. Beyond the glass door leading to the owner's bedroom, the wall of cabinetry continued in a storage wall separating bedroom from corridor.

↓
Room 606, Royal Hotel, SAS House,
Copenhagen, 1955–60. The room is deco-
rated with examples of the furniture that
Jacobsen designed especially for the
SAS House. The rigid frame of the two-seat
Series 3300 sofa, originally designed for
the air terminal, creates a strong contrast
with the organic chairs that were created
for the Royal Hotel.

Much of the sensual delight of Room 606 stems from the juxtaposition of contrasting materials and modes of production. While the windows expose the industrially produced curtain wall of the hotel, the wenge paneling that is the interior equivalent was assembled in a woodworker's shop. The furniture in 606 unites these opposing methods of production in single objects that reflect Jacobsen's synthesis of industry and craft. Molded by machine and covered by hand, his sculpted chairs were small proofs of the blend of technology and tradition that gave the SAS House its timeless character.

The largest of the room's chairs is the Ægget (Egg) a high-backed lounge chair originally designed for the hotel lobby and also installed in the guest rooms. With its flaring shell and swiveling base, the Egg serves as both throne and refuge. Nearby, the low Svane (Swan) chair combines a deep seat with high armrests that wrap the sitter. Between Egg and Swan sits the FH 3515, one of the low tables that Jacobsen designed for the building; its top is wenge veneer to match the room's woodwork. In front of the wall-mounted dressing tables, the shallow bowl of the Dråben (Drop) chair rests on a quartet of splayed steel legs, completing the original furniture scheme. A two-seat sofa from Series 3300, which furnished the air terminal, has been added to create a representative sample of Jacobsen's designs for the building. The sofa and all the chairs except for the Drop are of recent production. All of the pieces have been covered in a brightly colored fabric that contrasts with Jacobsen's original palette of muted hues. Nonetheless, their essential forms and many of their details have remained constant and preserve the play of light and volume that Jacobsen intended.

For all of his tendencies toward *Gesamtkunstwerk*, Jacobsen viewed architecture and furniture design as distinct disciplines, and the freestanding furnishings in 606 are independent objects

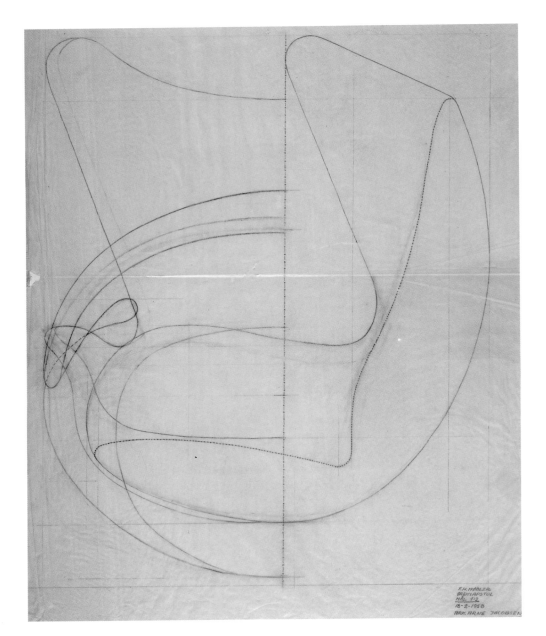

←

Drawing of the Egg chair, 1958. Jacobsen designed his furniture using full-scale models and then translating the forms into two-dimensional drawings. This drawing combines a frontal view with a section of the chair and illustrates the undulating curve that unites the seat and the back into a single form.

↓

Turkis, woven wool upholstery fabric for the C. Olesen company (Cotil 925), 1959. This fabric was used to cover the Egg and Swan chairs in the hotel rooms. The complex pattern of twisting lines resembled aquatic plants and combined the botanical material of Jacobsen's early textiles with the abstraction of his mature work.

↘

Royal, woven wool upholstery fabric for the C. Olesen company (Cotil 990), 1959. Jacobsen covered most of the furniture in the SAS House with solid-colored wool fabrics. This selection of fabrics, recently reissued by Dansk Art Weaving A/S, illustrates the subtle hues of blue and green that defined Jacobsen's palette.

that reflect his approach. While the low table serves as a horizontal counterpart to the paneling, the sculptural forms of the chairs provide a vivid contrast to the right angles of the room. This contrast has often been cited as an attempt to soften the austere quality of the architecture, but there is no evidence that Jacobsen felt the need to temper his own creation. In fact, these differences in form illustrate his sensitivity to scale and the importance he placed on the human body determining the contours of an object.

Jacobsen's minimalist approach—the reduction of form and the use of a limited set of materials—was grounded in the functionalist philosophy of the early modern movement. Functionalism dictated that form was a result of utility and the logic of production, but Jacobsen leavened this potentially arid equation with his own set of priorities, in which beauty was a primary function.

These vintage chairs illustrate Jacobsen's essential formula of a sculpted foam shell supported by a metal base. This rare example of the Drop chair with copper-plated legs was one of forty special models created for the snack bar of the Royal Hotel. The Swan and the Egg chairs share a pedestal that combines column and feet in a cast-aluminum stem.
←
Egg chair, 1958.
↙
Swan chair, 1958.
↓
Drop chair, 1958.

Throughout his career, Jacobsen used architectural commissions as opportunities to design new types of seating. Before the SAS House, the most important of these designs had been the Myren (Ant), a stacking chair of laminated wood that he developed for the lunchroom of a pharmaceutical factory. The complex mix of programs and spaces at the SAS House required a range of furnishings, and Jacobsen responded with six new types of seating and a collection of low tables. Like the lighting and textiles he designed for the building, the furniture served both functional and decorative ends. This latter role was especially evident in the coordination between finishes, such as the Drop chairs in the snack bar, whose copper-plated legs complemented the copper-plated hanging lamps, and the Swan chairs with bronzed bases used amid the Douglas fir panels of the Panorama Room.

The new chairs for the SAS House combined Jacobsen's ongoing pursuit of minimal form with a new process for forming synthetic rubber. In the mid-1950s, Henry W. Klein, a Norwegian industrial designer and recent graduate of the Academy of Arts in Copenhagen, developed a technique for steam-molding polystyrene beads into chair seats. By 1957, Klein and a group of investors had set up Plastmobler A/S and began licensing the process to factories around the world. The Danish licensee was Fritz Hansen Eftf., the manufacturer of the Ant, and it is likely that the company's contact with Jacobsen was immediate. Anecdotal accounts suggest that he was initially discouraged by the amorphous material, but he eventually realized that the molded foam would allow him to transcend the structural limits of laminated wood.

Each of the major spaces of the SAS House was furnished with a distinctive type of new seating. The first of these chairs was the Swan, originally intended for the air terminal and eventually installed throughout the Royal Hotel. The Swan represents a transition between materials; the deep dish of the shell had its origins in Jacobsen's attempts to produce a one-piece armchair of laminated wood. This connection is explicit in a 1958 drawing and model for a plywood shell with flaring arms and a curved back that resembles the Seven Series chairs of 1955. The Swan's shell features an undulating profile that exploited the tight curves and deep bowl made possible by the molding process. From the high point at the top of the chair, the curved back descends to a narrow waist that recalls the Ant, before rising and billowing out into deep armrests that are reunited along the front edge of the seat. Early versions of the Swan were outfitted with legs of laminated teak that mimicked the steel legs of the Ant and Seven chairs. After the design of the Egg in 1959, Jacobsen developed a new base of cast aluminum that allowed the chair to swivel and extended the basic formula of separate base and shell that had been established by the Ant.

While the Swan retained traces of Jacobsen's wood chairs, the Egg was an autonomous creation that maximized the sculptural properties of the new material. Designed for the Royal Hotel lobby, the Egg is a high-backed lounge chair in which seat, back, and arms are united by three sets of sweeping curves. It is defined by a spherical volume whose interior is hollowed out

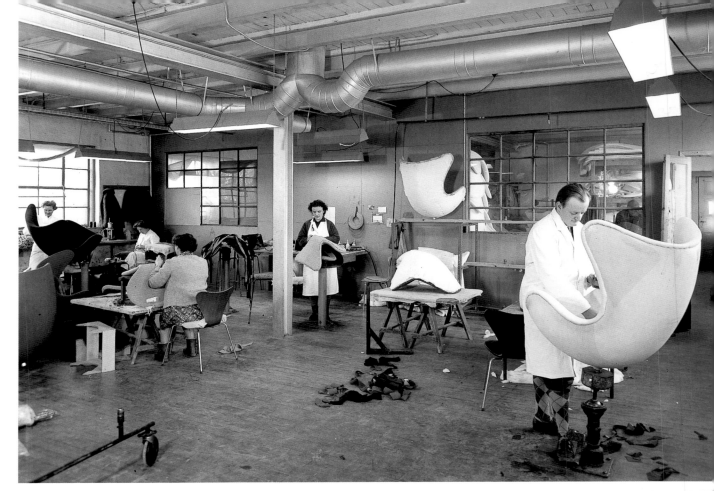

ritz Hansen Eftf. factory, c. 1959. The
olded-foam chairs that Jacobsen de-
gned for the hotel were covered in
ather or fabric by a labor-intensive
rocess of hand-tailoring. In the case of
ather covering, damp skins were pinned
to place and allowed to dry over the
rm of the shell, prior to the final needle-
ork. This process, which is still followed,
lows a typical craftsman to finish six to
even chairs per week.

ock-up of the Egg chair, c. 1959. This
berglass-and-foam-rubber model was
ne of the working prototypes for the Egg.
the final design, it would be rotated
rward to provide an upright posture, and
e points of the back would be straight-
ned to reinforce the effect of a continuous
hell. The base of bent steel tubing sug-
ests that the pedestal was unresolved
ntil late in the design process.

bby of the Royal Hotel, 1960. Jacobsen
esigned the Egg specifically for the hotel
bby and arranged seating groups to pro-
de islands of repose. This image is the
nly record of a pair of Egg sofas that
ere made for the hotel but never put into
eneral production.

↑
Panorama Room, Royal Hotel. At the top of
the hotel tower, a lounge offered continuous views in three directions over the city
and the Øresund to Sweden. The room was
furnished with special models of the Swan
chair outfitted with bronzed bases that
complemented the brass-plated Royal
pendants.

↓
Model of the Swan prototype, c. 1955. The
painted cardboard model was created during the design process that would lead to
the Seven Series of laminated wood
armchairs. Jacobsen had hoped to provide
a shell that combined seat, back, and
arms in a single form, but the curves of
the armrests exceeded the laminated
wood's structural capabilities.

↓
Drawing of the Swan prototype, 1958.
Three years after the conception of the
cardboard model, the revolutionary technique of molded synthetic rubber provided
Jacobsen with the proper material for his
one-piece armchair.

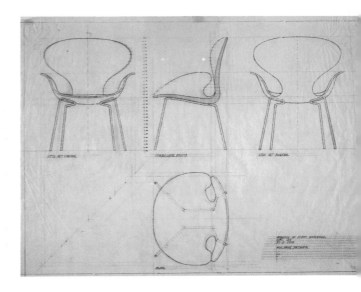

create a gentle bowl for the occupant and a sculpted back for lumbar support. At the SAS House, the Egg was covered with leather or woven fabric and joined by a hand-stitched seam that served as the only ornamentation.

All of the hotel's molded chairs were constructed of three layers of material: a shell of fiberglass that served as a base, an inner layer of foam padding that tapered to the edges of the shell, and a hand-finished covering. Jacobsen believed that direct contact with materials was essential to design, and, in advance of the work at the factory, he searched for his forms using full-size plaster models he and his assistants carved and refined with saw, file, and sandpaper. After this modeling process, the final sets of curves were charted in 1:1 scale drawings to assist the factory in developing its production equipment.

Jacobsen took every opportunity to exert aesthetic control and to create new forms and materials. He covered his furniture with fabrics of his own design. While his curtains for the hotel were characterized by geometric patterns, the furniture coverings used muted colors and subtle textures to create surfaces that rewarded touch as well as vision. Most of these fabrics were woven exclusively for the project and today survive only on a handful of chairs and in period photographs. Jacobsen intended to cover the Swan chair in Regn, a pattern of colored drops on a contrasting background. The pattern was manufactured in eight color schemes that, owing to its reversible nature, yielded sixteen possible combinations. In the guest rooms, the Egg, Swan, and Drop chairs were covered in a multicolored field of twisted yarns that resembled river grasses and suited the continuous forms of the chairs. The Egg, the Swan, and the Series 3300 were intended for mass production, and for them Jacobsen created a range of solid-colored wool fabrics, Royal, that combined slight differences in the colors of the warp and the weft yarns to create a field of subtle texture. Royal's fourteen-color palette was heavily weighted toward the earth tones and subtle shades of green that reiterated the naturalism at the heart of Jacobsen's work.

The Swan and the Egg were the signature furnishings of the SAS House, but they were not intended to be used in every area of the building. Most effective alone or in small groups, the chairs' voluptuous shells tended to dominate their surroundings, while their deep seats encouraged repose rather than an upright position. Jacobsen designed a pair of smaller, less formal chairs for the Royal Hotel, the Pot and the Drop, which were used in a wider variety of spaces.

Gryden (Pot) was a gentle bowl of molded foam that curled out to provide armrests. Supported by a set of crossed steel legs, the shell was separated from the base by small spurs that articulated Jacobsen's binary equation of body and pedestal. In the winter garden, the chairs were covered with a rich green fabric that provided splashes of color above the earth tones of the carpets and echoed the foliage within the surrounding walls. In the Orchid Bar, the Pot chairs were supplemented with a unique Pot sofa cantilevered from the wall on steel brackets. A single Pot also appeared on each floor of the hotel tower. Covered in brown leather, it was placed in a niche

→
Winter garden of the Royal Hotel. This
image from 1960 records the winter
garden in its textile and chromatic splen-
dor. The hotel management, preferring
conventional modes of decorum, had covered the rosewood tables with tablecloths.
The layering of interior views and the
contrasting effects of lighting resulted in
the most spectacular of the interior landscapes that filled the SAS House.

↙
Pot chair, 1959. The Pot chair was designed for the winter garden of the Royal
Hotel. This vintage example features the
original green wool fabric that Jacobsen
selected as a complement to the hanging
foliage that lined the double-glass walls
of the room.

Seating area of the Royal Hotel snack bar
The gentle bowls of the Drop chair provide
a complement to the Royal pendant lamp
that lit the alcoves along the wall separating the hotel from the air terminal.
These alcoves were framed by oak lattices
that reiterated Jacobsen's use of patterned
screens to subdivide his interiors.

opposite the elevators to provide guests with a meeting point.

The smallest of the molded chairs was the Dråben (Drop), an abstract sliver of molded foam. Designed for the hotel snack bar and used also in the guest rooms, the Drop featured a shallow seat and a tapering back. In the snack bar, the Drop was covered in chestnut brown leather and had copper-plated legs that matched the hanging AJ Royal lamps. In the guest rooms, where Drop chairs served the dressing tables, they were covered in one of Jacobsen's subtle fabrics and had chrome-plated legs. While the other chairs featured a clear separation between shell and base, the Drop was supported on splayed legs that entered the underside without transition.

Jacobsen completed his set of furnishings for the SAS House with a series of low tables used in all the communal spaces as well as in the guest rooms, where they served as coffee tables and desks. The basic components were two distinct cast-aluminum bases, one derived from American Shaker dining tables and available in two heights, the other a modified version of the base of the Egg and Swan chairs. The bases were crowned with round or rectangular tops covered in wenge, rosewood, or blue plastic laminate, depending on their location. In the winter garden, round tables with rosewood tops were surrounded with Pot chairs, while the same tables in the Panorama Room had tops of Douglas fir to match the wall paneling.

In addition to the chairs and tables used in various locations, Jacobsen designed seating for specific locations. The most striking of this eclectic group was the Giraffe, a high-backed dining chair for the hotel restaurant that mixed form and material to ambiguous effect. The Giraffe combined the fiberglass shell that was the foundation of the molded-foam shells with legs of laminated beech that had been developed for an all-wood dining chair in 1955. One hundred twenty chairs were produced for the hotel's trio of dining rooms, as well as six Giraffe sofas, 140 centimeters wide, that were used as banquettes on the sidewalls of the central dining room. Along the edge of the lightly padded shell, which was tapered to allow easier access for the wait-staff, strips of elm were applied to protect the fiberglass at its thinnest point. The Giraffe was intended as an integrated form that used wood to establish visual unity between the base and the shell. Beyond the matching of materials, the curving legs repeat the sweep of the shell as it narrows from armrest to back. In spite of this repetition of curves and the graceful form of both shell and legs, the Giraffe has an effect of applied decoration absent from the molded chairs.

Much of the formal power of Jacobsen's most original chairs lies in their integrity as self-contained forms—their complex curvature and tension with the surrounding space renders any applied decoration redundant. At the same time, these chairs are articulated as binary equations, with a shell and a base of different materials and forms. While the hand-stitching along the edge of the Swan and its offspring ties the inner and outer surfaces into a continuous body, the wood edging of the Giraffe splits the shell into distinct surfaces that undermines the tension between shell and base.

↑
Main dining room of the Royal Hotel. The Giraffe chairs were arranged around rectangular tables (FH 4605) with laminated legs matching those of the chairs.

↖ ↖
Giraffe chair, 1959. Jacobsen designed this high-backed dining chair for the restaurant of the Royal Hotel. The Giraffe combined the laminated wood legs developed for the Grand Prix chair with a lightly padded shell that was profiled in elm to protect its thin edges.

↖
Detail of the Giraffe chair. Jacobsen created a stain resistant fabric that would harmonize with the green carpet and gray green ceiling of the hotel's second floor.

←
Giraffe office chair, 1960. In the management offices of the hotel, the Giraffe shell was supported by a cast-aluminum base that had been designed for the Swan armchair.

Passenger hall of the SAS air terminal. The
hall was furnished with rows of Series
3300 chairs and sofas covered in a dark
blue wool.

→
Series 3300 armchair and sofa, 1956. The
Series 3300 used a single cushion as the
basis for a seating system of potentially
infinite length. The key to this flexibility
was the separation of frame and structure.
A wood skeleton concealed within the upholstery supported the cushions, creating
a rigid form that was inserted into the
tubular-steel armature.

↘ ↘
Drawing of the 3300 armchair, 1956.
Originally developed as a modular system
of chairs and sofas for Rødovre Town Hall,
the 3300 series was used to furnish
the passenger hall and areas of the Royal
Hotel. In the lower-left corner of the
drawing, a detail of the steel tubing illustrates the careful articulation of seat
from supporting structure.

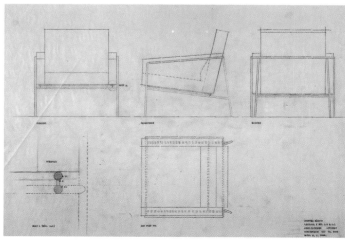

Jacobsen's characteristic creation of variations on a single form is exhibited in the special sofas that were developed for the Royal Hotel. This rare Giraffe sofa was installed along the walls of the main dining room in late 1960. A pair of Swan sofas, eventually put into general production in 2001, were installed in the hotel's second-floor sitting rooms in 1960. The Egg sofa, originally made for the hotel lobby, was recreated by Fritz Hansen A/S in 2002 to commemorate Jacobsen's centennial.

↑ ↑
Giraffe sofa, 1959.
↑
Egg sofa, 1959.
↗
Swan sofa (FH 3321), 1959.

↓
Tables designed for the Royal Hotel (from left to right: FH 3515, FH 3513, FH 3512). Jacobsen complemented his chairs with a range of tables covered in teak, rosewood, or oak, depending on the setting. While the low table used in the guest rooms featured an aluminum base inspired by American Shaker designs, the round tables in the public areas were supported on cast-aluminum variants of the bases for the Egg and Swan chairs.

Jacobsen had originally imagined the Swan as the principal seating in the air terminal, but he eventually reworked an earlier design to create a system of modular seating for that space. In the terminal's central hall, orderly rows of upholstered chairs and two-seat sofas, the Series 3300, provided seating for sixty passengers. One floor below, a darkened "meditation" room furnished with the same series provided a refuge for passengers with long layovers. In contrast to the singular forms of the molded chairs and the Giraffe, the Series 3300 was a modular system that could be extended to create sofas of variable length. The prototype for the series was the sofa designed for the public waiting areas of the Rødovre Town Hall. In response to the variety of travelers expected at the SAS House, Jacobsen used this sofa as the basis for rows of seating that could accommodate individuals or groups while still providing a uniform appearance.

In contrast to the molded chairs that clearly separated seat from base, the 3300 Series consisted of an upholstered body set into a frame of steel tubes. While the continuous tubes of the front legs follow the profile of the armrest and back, the stretchers and back legs are canted back for added stability. The series is also distinguished by a dichotomy of form and construction that is consistent with Jacobsen's emphasis on form over structure. While the steel frame supports the seat body, the slender tubes are inadequate to span the width of the sofas. By concealing the structure of the seat—a traditional wood frame—within the padded body, he was able to maintain the visual distinction between frame and infill that accounts for the visual delicacy and formal tension of the series.

Amid this array of new designs, Jacobsen adapted one of his earlier plywood chairs to provide stools along the counter in the snack bar. Originally designed for the youngest students at the Munkegård School, the 3102, popularly known as the Tongue, was developed as part of a standard desk set. Jacobsen supported the shell on a quartet of steel legs similar to that of the Drop chair. Enlarged to adult dimensions and covered in gray leather, the Tongue was installed on a swiveling steel base that provided diners with easy access to the bar while allowing passage to the tables beyond the winter garden. While these dozen stools were unique within the hotel, their inclusion is emblematic of Jacobsen's reworking of a repertoire of basic forms.

↓
Munkegård School, Gentofte, 1948–57.
The classrooms of the school were accom
modated with vestibules that served as
coatrooms and provided space for art
lessons and other small group activities.
To accommodate the pupils, Jacobsen
developed a series of laminated wood
chairs—including the FH 3105 pictured
here—scaled to the children and designed
to provide lower-back support. A full-
scale version was produced for the faculty.

The new designs for the SAS House were the product of Jacobsen's thirty-year-long exploration into the essential form of the chair. Before World War II, he had worked with woodworkers and upholsterers to produce variations on traditional types of seating. After 1950, craft was supplanted by technology, when new industrial processes of bending and laminating materials contributed to the creation of radically new forms. This evolution mirrored the transformation of Jacobsen's architecture and highlights the catalytic role of technology in his career. While Henry Klein's innovative method of molding styropore pellets provided the technique, the material was like clay, without structural properties, and did not lend itself to any particular shape. To turn method into form Jacobsen drew upon his own history of chair designs.

Jacobsen's first chair was constructed in 1925, while he was still a student. Exhibited that year at the landmark Exposition des Arts Décoratifs in Paris, the chair was awarded a silver medal and provided Jacobsen with his first public recognition. A decade later the upholstered lounge chair and sofa he created for the H.I.K. Tennis Club introduced the dramatic curves that eventually defined the chairs of the SAS House. In 1935, Jacobsen also furnished the Bellevue theater and restaurant with a variety of seating that reflected the varied influences of his early career and his own attempts at creating distinctive modern forms.

Rows of upholstered seats in the Bellevue theater hall were connected by undulating ribbons of laminated wood that displayed the persistent influence of Erik Gunnar Asplund. In the restaurant,

the lightweight dining chairs of steam-bent beech with backs inspired by traditional Chinese *quanyi* chairs recalled the encouragement to use foreign models by Kaare Klint, who believed that the pertinent questions of design were universal and had been solved repeatedly in different cultures and eras. The organic stools of leather and steel around the bar combined Jacobsen's own interests in organic form with the bent steel tubing that had become a hallmark of modernity through the work of Marcel Breuer and Mart Stam.

These very different designs can be considered as prototypes for the later stages of Jacobsen's furniture design. While the dining chairs were made at the Fritz Hansen factory, Jacobsen would soon develop new wood chairs with the cabinetmakers who were the backbone of Denmark's furniture industry. In the 1950s, long after he had emerged from the shadow of Asplund, Jacobsen would return to laminated wood to create his most enduring design, a lightweight stacking chair that would become the best-selling chair of the twentieth century.

The least resolved of the Bellevue designs, the bar stool, can be considered an important precedent for the Egg chair. While the backrest, like the upholstered chairs for the tennis club and the bank branches, exhibits an early use of organic form and a continuing appreciation of the English wing chair, it was the stool's base that had a direct influence. Twenty years before he was confronted with the problem of creating adequate bases for his self-contained shells, Jacobsen found the beginning of a solution in the bundled

→
Bellevue theater, Klampenborg, 1935–37.
In this theater, which was part of a summer resort complex north of Copenhagen,
Jacobsen paid homage to the work of Erik
Gunnar Asplund. Characterized by their
simple curvature, the rows of laminated
beech seats provided both visual and
acoustic relief in the large performance
hall. These seats would serve as the foundation for Jacobsen's later contributions
to modern furniture design.
↓
Summer dining room of the Bellevue
theater. While the curving top rails of the
beech wood dining chairs echo the seats
of the theater, the scrolled backs are
derived from traditional Chinese models.
↘
View of the bar in the Bellevue theater.
These highly stylized bar stools would be
little more than a curiosity were it not for
their catalytic role in the development of
Jacobsen's later designs. Twenty-five
years after conception, both the curving
back and the bundled steel legs were
reinterpreted in the Egg and in the chairs
for St. Catherine's College.

teel tubes that splay into individual feet as they meet the floor. In 958, these tubes would be joined into a column of cast aluminum ith projecting spurs and delicate fluting.

The most comprehensive commissions of Jacobsen's early areer were the town halls in Aarhus and Søllerød. Completed etween 1939 and 1942 by Jacobsen and his collaborators, Erik øller in Aarhus and Flemming Lassen in Søllerød, both buildings ere furnished with special furniture, fixtures, and woodwork that roduced an integrated environment at every scale of experience. his emphasis on the total environment was a product not only f an artistic vision, but also of a lack of suitable furnishings. The anish furniture industry was still in its infancy, while importing oods was economically and politically unfeasible. At the same me, though, Danish craft culture was highly evolved, with a large umber of workshops producing high-quality items in wood nd metal. To circumvent the shortage of modern furnishings, acobsen and his fellow modernist architects, including Vilhelm auritzsen and Kay Fisker, worked with craftsmen to create rniture that bridged the cultural divide between traditional tech- que and contemporary form.

Søllerød Town Hall's varied program of public spaces, unicipal offices, and ceremonial rooms gave Jacobsen and assen the opportunity to create a set of chairs that presaged the ariations-on-a-theme of the SAS House's molded seating. Work- g with cabinetmakers at Rud. Rasmussen Snedkerieri, the archi- cts designed a trio of armchairs that used differences in materials

and detailing to reflect gradations of function and ceremony. In the council chamber, the curving desk of the town councilors was com- plemented by armchairs and writing surfaces covered in matching pigskin. The chair's broad backs and wide armrests constitute a subtle reworking of English wing chairs; their flowing curves would later reappear in the Egg. Stripped-down versions of these chairs in the tax assessment offices displayed their frames and were covered with leather along their vulnerable edges. Elsewhere in the building, armchairs that combined laminated and joined wood— variations on the councilors' chairs designed for Aarhus Town Hall—were outfitted with padded cushions of pigskin.

The chairs Jacobsen created after 1950 are potent examples of his willingness to embrace technology to realize aesthetic goals. The first of these was a stackable wood chair designed for a factory lunchroom in 1951. While completing a renovation of an insulin plant for the Novo Company, Jacobsen searched for a light- weight chair that could be pushed under the tables for ease of cleaning and stacked for compact storage. Unable to find a suit- able model, he chose to design one himself. Working with full- scale models, Jacobsen developed a shell of laminated beech veneers that combined seat and back in a single curved form. On the underside, three legs of bent steel tube were joined by a cen- tral plate and separated from the wood by rubber bumpers that gave added spring to the pliable shell. To prevent the wood veneers from curling at the transition between seat and back—the point of maximum tension—Jacobsen cut into the shell, producing the

ax assessor's office, Søllerød Town Hall,
øllerød, 1939–42. In the offices of the
own hall, the basic frame of the coun-
ilor's chair was reused, reserving the
eather covering for the most exposed
dges. On the desks, a built-in brass lamp
erved as a prototype for the multipurpose
sor fixture that would be used through-
ut the SAS House.

eception hall chair, Søllerød Town Hall.
he simple side chair of turned and lami-
ated beech was a distilled version of the
ore elaborate armchairs. Although the
hairs reflected differences in function
nd status, they shared a common set of
rms and structural principles.

ouncilor's chair. While the basic division
etween leather-covered seat and tapered
ood legs is straightforward, Jacobsen's
esire for dramatic form is apparent in the
aring armrests.

ew of the council chamber. Jacobsen
nd Møller treated the furniture as an
nsemble of woodwork, with armchairs,
riting surfaces, and modesty panels
vered in natural pigskin.

istinctive profile that gave the chair its name. Introduced in 1952, ne Ant was the first of Jacobsen's mature furniture designs and ne basis of the plywood chairs that would continue to occupy him hroughout his life.

The self-contained shell of the Ant did not accommodate rms, however, and Jacobsen soon began working on a second aminated-wood chair that had armrests and, not incidentally, an-wered the skeptics who preferred that a chair have four legs. To naintain the minimal composition of wood shell and steel base, acobsen extended the back legs above the height of the seat and ent them forward to support armrests of laminated wood. He also eworked the shape of the shell to accommodate the projecting teel tubes, easing the curves and widening the seat. The result was ne basic shell of the Syveren (Seven) series, Jacobsen's most ersatile furniture design. While the foundation of the series was ne armchair, it was equally useful and ultimately more popular ithout arms. The Seven could also be combined with a variety of upports, including a swivel base with wheels for offices and a fixed edestal for lecture halls.

This persistent pursuit of variations on a single form eflected both Jacobsen's minimal aesthetic and the search for ssential types that had been inculcated in him at the Royal cademy. Throughout his career, he sought typical solutions, dis-llations of form and material, that could be altered to suit a range f settings and a variety of functions. Thus all the wood elements f a chair would be combined into a single form, and the metal

elements would be reduced to their minimal dimensions. From this perspective, the zenith of his plywood chairs was the 4130, a dining chair introduced at the 1957 Milan Triennale, where it was garnered the highest award. This chair, known as the Grand Prix, combined a distinctive shell and a set of laminated-beech legs, cruciform in section to reduce their visual weight, into a single object that fused form and material.

As much as any aspect of Jacobsen's output, the laminated chairs illustrate his synthesis of natural materials and abstract form. Well trained in both the physiological effects and structural limitations of wood, Jacobsen used machinery to reconcile the apparent gap between nature and technology. In these chairs, as in his buildings of the 1950s, we are confronted with an abstract treat-ment of the natural world.

Following the completion of the SAS House, Jacobsen, perhaps recognizing that he had exhausted the sculptural poten-tial of molded styropore foam, returned to the formal possibilities of laminated wood. To be certain, there were further variations on the themes of padded throne and modular seating, including the Ox chair (1961–65), and the Series 3600 for the Mainz Town Hall. But the majority of Jacobsen's subsequent furniture designs pursued the ideal of an entire chair in a single material.

In early 1960, as the SAS House was nearing completion, Jacobsen began work on the first new residential college con-structed at Oxford since the seventeenth century, St. Catherine's. To create a harmonious effect among the residential buildings, the

↑

Employee canteen, Novo Nordisk A/S factory, Copenhagen, 1934, remodeled 1952.
Designed in 1952, the Ant chair (FH 3100)
was Jacobsen's breakthrough in furniture
design, establishing the template for most
of his future chairs. Jacobsen designed a
range of tables, both circular and rectangular, to complement the steel legs and
suspended wood shell.

↓

Connection between the seat and legs of
the FH 3207. A set of rubber bumpers
separated the wood shell and steel legs,
allowing them to function as independent
structures and increasing their resiliency.
↓ ↓

Fritz Hansen Eftf. furniture factory, c. 1957.

With the critical and commercial success
of the Ant, Jacobsen soon began work on
laminated wood armchair. When the pursuit of a single shell was proved unfeasibl
he settled for a combination of steel arms
and wooden armrests. The resulting 3207
armchair was the basis of the Seven
series, yet it was quickly supplemented by
versions without arms: The 3107 became
the most successful chair of the twentiet
century (eventually selling more than six
million units), and the 3105, originally
designed for the Munkegård School, was
also soon put into general production.
All the shells were available in a range
of finishes and upholstery options,
with special office versions featuring
adjustable seats and wheels.

→

Seven series (FH 3207 and variant), 1955
↘

Seven series (FH 3107 and variant), 1955
↘ ↘

Laminated-wood chair (FH 3105 and
variant), 1955.

dining and lecture buildings, and the library, Jacobsen devised a single structural motif, a modular system of exposed long-span beams and cruciform columns, all of precast concrete, with a surface that one critic compared to marble. On the basis of the SAS House, Jacobsen was granted responsibility for the college's furnishings, too. These objects would be his last significant body of furniture design.

Jacobsen equipped the college with Swan chairs and a mixture of old and new lighting fixtures, but he also worked with Fritz Hansen A/S to create two sets of furnishings that reflected the social conventions of a traditional Oxford college. In the top-lit cavern of the dining hall, where students dined on rows of wood benches (later replaced by Seven chairs), the dons and fellows of St. Catherine's occupied a raised dais, the High Table, that was outfitted with laminated-wood dining chairs. These ceremonial chairs—single shells of laminated wood, veneered in oak, on columns of bentwood legs—consolidated Jacobsen's experience with the Grand Prix chair and the stools of the Bellevue bar. From the front and back, the High chairs appeared to be floating rectangles of oak, while a side view revealed Jacobsen's response to ergonomics and his mastery of line. Prototypes of a second chair for the faculty, an office chair with undulating armrests that was one of his most delicate designs were also constructed. Like the Grand Prix, the Low chair integrated form and material through technology that let Jacobsen overcome the limits of the natural material. These wood chairs formed the basis of the Oxford series, a collection of padded chairs with steel bases that were manufactured for the college and commercially available until the late 1980s.

Jacobsen also created furniture for the college's 268 undergraduate rooms. A pair of chairs and a low ottoman-table were constructed of bent oak members spanned by planes of plywood and padding. Grooves articulated the structures of the frames and highlighted the wooden members that provided lateral support. At the far end of the rooms, opposite the window wall, Jacobsen made the most of the limited space by integrating built-in bookcases and sliding beds.

Jacobsen continued to design chairs in the final years of his life, but the tension between industrial production and human anatomy that characterize his now classic designs had dissipated. His energies were absorbed by large-scale architectural commissions, particularly the new building for Denmark's National Bank, and by industrial design projects for hollowware and plumbing fittings, which allowed him to combine geometric abstraction and tactile experience on a very small scale. The renovation of an old farm in Tisso into his summer retreat and the development of a system of modular prefabricated houses were other personal creative outlets. As a result, the furniture designs that followed St. Catherine's lacked the clarity of his designs from the previous decade and were likely put into production on the basis of Jacobsen's stature and earlier successes.

However, Jacobsen did continue his pursuit of unified form in the design for an office chair that would be entirely of plastic.

↑
Dining room with Grand Prix chairs
(FH 4130) and matching table (FH 4600),
Round House, Odden, 1957. A short dis-
tance from the 1943 Fish Smokehouse,
Jacobsen constructed a house with a
circular plan for the manager of the Odden
Fiskerøgeri. The Grand Prix chair reiterated
Jacobsen's minimalist tendencies by
rendering the entire chair in laminated
beech, covered with either teak or beech
face veneers.

St. Catherine's College High Table dining
chair, 1963. Jacobsen's exploration of all-
wood chairs continued with this powerful
essay in sinuous lines.
←
Dining hall of St. Catherine's College,
Oxford, 1960-64. In the dining hall, the
Dons and Fellows of the college were
seated on a raised dais, the High Table.
Totemic chairs of laminated oak defined
an intimate environment within the
cavernous space.

↑ ↗
Prototype armchair for St. Catherine's
College, 1963. Created for the faculty, this
all-wood armchair was one of the most
delicate designs of Jacobsen's career.
The shallow curve of the seat and the
tapering of the armrests as they extend
outward typify Jacobsen's nuanced
approach to form.
→
Armchair (FH 3271) from the Oxford
series, 1965. The laminated wood chairs
designed for the college were the basis
for the Oxford Series of swiveling chairs
that combined upholstered shells with a
variety of aluminum bases.

Exterior of a residential building,
St. Catherine's College, Oxford, 1959–64.
The students live and study in a pair of
three-story structures that form the edges
of the college. Aluminum window walls
are set between walls of precast concrete.

Interior of typical bedroom at St. Catherine's
College. Jacobsen designed a typical set
of furnishings that included desk and
lounge chairs, a square ottoman-table,
and a wall-mounted desk.

Detail of the connection between the frame
and seat of the St. Catherine's lounge
chair. Jacobsen treated the laminated-
wood structur of the students' furnishings
with the same attention to detail that he
lavished on the building.

Plaster model of untitled office chair,
1970–71. Jacobsen's last design for furniture, left unfinished at his death, was
a one-piece office chair that would have
been molded in plastic. In contrast to
his previous designs, in which seat and
back were joined into a single shell, the
back of this final chair is mounted on a
stem that grows from the columnar base.

Left unfinished and untitled at his death, a plaster model preserves
the confrontation between the rational world of production and
Jacobsen's personal vocabulary of form. It was this collision that
distinguished him as one of the great form givers of the twentieth
century, an agent of a transcendent modernity who worked the seam
between the industrial and the natural worlds.

Just as the SAS House gathered the themes of Jacobsen's career into a single setting, it itself was designed as a cumulative experience of forms. It was through the details, the carpets and door handles, the ashtrays and signage, that the ensemble of architecture and furnishings became more than the sum of its parts. While this *Gesamtkunstwerk* was experienced as a continuous setting, with each object designed to the same standard of beauty and workmanship, the contrasts between these objects, large and small, curved and straight, allowed them to be experienced as individual artifacts, each taking the form appropriate to its use. Jacobsen's use of form was characterized by a rigorous correspondence between shape and scale. He consistently treated things larger than the body as geometric components in a larger framework, while the objects that hold the body, or are held in the hand, employ the tightly controlled curves that constituted his personal geometry.

The elements of the SAS House—from building to furniture to objects—displayed a direct correspondence between scale, form, and technique. The geometric frames of the curtain wall were constructed of mass-produced components; the voluptuous chairs and delicate light fixtures were shaped in molds and presses and finished by hand; at the smallest scale, the objects were craft products, handmade by traditional artisans. In Room 606, the door hardware—the handles and locksets that connect the vestibule with the bedroom and bathrooms—provides the last evidence of these utilitarian objects designed by Jacobsen for the SAS House.

The AJ-grebet (handle) was designed in 1956 for the hardware manufacturer Carl F. Petersen, where it was cast in white bronze and then ground and polished by hand. Today, the handle is made in nickel-plated brass and offered with either a rose or an escutcheon, and an optional thumb turn. Jacobsen had been designing door hardware since the Bellevue theater of 1935, and

Room 606, Royal Hotel, SAS House, Copenhagen, 1955–60. The interior doors of the room are equipped with the white bronze handle that Jacobsen designed as an extension of the body. Mounted on a slender escutcheon, the handle has a circular thumb turn thickened at the edges to ensure an easy grip.

↙

AJ-handle, Room 606. The handle combines a curved lever and a cylindrical stem into a single form that resolves the intersection of hand and door. The white bronze resists discoloration and conceals fingerprints, minimizing the need for polishing.

↙ ↙ ↓

Handle production at the Carl F. Petersen factory. The handles were cast on a stem before being ground to a consistent surface. Even as Jacobsen embraced mass fabrication, his aesthetic of refined surfaces and intricate detailing required hand-finishing in the final stages of production. In its combination of machinery and handwork, the handle's manufacturing process mirrored that of the molded-foam chairs.

subsequent objects, for the Aarhus and Søllerød town halls and the Munkegård School, the strict geometry had given way to more ergonomic designs. The handle in 606 is a study in contrasting curves, with a sweeping lever rising to fill the palm and a concave underside to accept the fingertips. Beyond their practical function, these pieces of hardware illuminate the role of the details in Jacobsen's program of total design and the importance of scale to his work.

↑
Glassware for the Royal hotel, 1960.
A selection of blown-glass stemware
exhibits Jacobsen's use of a single motif
in this case a delicate curve between ste
and bowl, to create a family of related
forms. Photographed in Strüwing's studio
this uncropped image shows Jacobsen
holding the cloth backdrop.

Jacobsen's *Gesamtkunstwerk* was completed in the restaurant of the Royal Hotel, where his collection of artifacts, from glassware to candleholders, celebrated the sensual and social pleasures of dining. The tabletop objects combined Jacobsen's personal language of form with traditional materials, particularly silver, which he valued for its lustrous finish. These designs were realized in collaboration with artisans at a host of traditional Danish manufacturers, all of them suppliers to the monarchy. While the contrast between an ultramodern setting and hand-made luxury goods may seem paradoxical, Jacobsen valued the craftsmen for their mastery of detailing and surface treatments. The combination of contemporary form and traditional material suggests that Jacobsen was attempting to create timeless artifacts, type-forms, which would enter the canon of Danish applied arts. He selected the most traditional service of Danish porce-lain to serve as the centerpiece for his own designs.

In 1755, following the discovery of white clay, kaolin, on the island of Bornholm, the Danish king Christian VII founded the Royal Copenhagen porcelain factory to insure a domestic supply of the "white gold" for the royal household. One of the earliest patterns to be produced there was the Saxisk Mønster Musselmodel, or Mussel, which was inspired by patterns from Meissen, Saxony, where the blue underglaze painting technique had been perfected in the 1730s. While the name Mussel referred to the fluted porcelain surface, which resembled the mollusk, the design was actually a stylized depiction of flowers that had originated in India. In the early 1800s, Mussel was produced in green and red, but cobalt blue remained the most popular color, becoming so synonymous with the design that it is popularly known as the "Blue-Fluted" pattern. It was this pattern that Jacobsen chose for the dinner service of his ultramodern hotel, but in the soft green version of the 1820s. He persuaded Royal Copenhagen to produce a special edition for the hotel.

Jacobsen's search for integrated forms and variations on a single shape are evident in the collections of glassware and cutlery he created for the SAS House between 1956 and 1958. At the A/S Kastrup Glassværks, located on a sandy island south of Copenhagen, glassblowers worked from Jacobsen's sketches to produce his Tulipan range of drinking glasses for the bar and restau-rant. While the standard photograph by Strüwing presents six pieces of stemware, an archival drawing, annotated with production numbers and capacity, illustrates the entirety of the collec-tion. Individually, the glasses are notable for graceful curves that combine base, stem, and bowl into a single form that fills the hand and accommodates varied lengths of fingers. While wine-glasses are fairly consistent in form, glasses for water, beer, spirits, and liqueurs usually vary widely in size and shape. By creating an assortment of vessels, Jacobsen insured guests would experience a consistent series of shapes over the course of an evening.

To surround the special Mussel dinner service, Jacobsen embarked on what was his most audacious, and controversial, design for the SAS House, a new line of flatware. To carry out the

↓
Private dining room, Royal Hotel.
The restaurant tables were set with an array of artifacts that Jacobsen had designed specifically for the restaurant. While he stopped short on designing new dishes, he specified a variation of the classic Mussel pattern that would reflect the palette of greens that pervaded the furniture and textiles. At the end of the table, the gold embroidery of the curtains reflected light from the recessed fixtures behind the valance and the Klokkelampe on each table.

work, he enlisted the craftsmen of A. Michelsen Solvsmedie, the venerable Danish silversmiths and crown jeweler. The company had a long tradition of working with architects to produce silver wares, including Thorvald Bindesbøll in the nineteenth century and Kay Fisker in the twentieth. This legacy was undoubtedly appealing to Jacobsen; he had been a student of Fisker at the Royal Academy, where he had also studied and measured a number of Bindesbøll's buildings.

Jacobsen's AJA flatware was a collection of eating utensils that abandoned conventional forms and ornament in favor of curving planes of stainless steel plated with silver. As an early sketch indicates, Jacobsen designed his utensils as gestural tools that would serve as lightweight extensions of the body. In spite of its radical appearance, the flatware, which had been carefully designed through the use of plaster models and hammered metal prototypes, was tailored to meet the needs of both hand and mouth. Like Jacobsen's door handle, the utensils fit easily into the hand and provided broad, flat surfaces for the fingertips, while the utensils narrowed where they would enter the mouth.

Traditionally, silverware has consisted of two distinct elements, a decorated handle and a functional head. This reflects the process of silversmithing and, in the case of the knife, the necessity of using a steel blade. Even stamped-steel utensils retain the traditional division between handle and head. By contrast, the forms of the AJA flatware corresponded to their manufacturing process and took advantage of the ability of stainless steel to provide thin, lightweight forms of enormous durability. Following the stamping process, the rough implements were tooled and ground to create the serrations on the knives and the points of the fork tines and to prepare the surface for the silver plating that served as the sole means of ornament. While traditional silver services were conceived of as a pattern that used a decorative motif to create a unified set of objects, Jacobsen's flatware was devoid of engraved or stamped decoration, relying on sets of gentle curves for visual harmony. In spite of this absence of ornament, the flatware followed the standard typology of specialized tools, including specific forks and spoons for the multiple courses of a formal dinner, as well as a host of specialized utensils such as fish knives, cold-cut forks, and cake servers. As a grace note and a reflection of his functionalist tendencies, Jacobsen completed the service with asymmetrical soup spoons for both the left and the right hands.

Jacobsen's flatware was the most radical of his excursions into the applied arts. The AJA flatware aroused the hostility of the hotel manager, who found it bizarre to look at and reported that guests found it difficult to use. The flatware also became an object of ridicule for the local newspapers, which were already suspicious of the unconventional forms of the building, its furnishings, and the level of luxury it offered. One of the papers published pictures of a hapless correspondent attempting to eat peas with one of Jacobsen's forks. The hotel soon replaced the flatware with a conventional pattern. However, the AJA (or AJ) line became a commercial success outside the hotel, and it is still in production, available in matte and polished stainless steel.

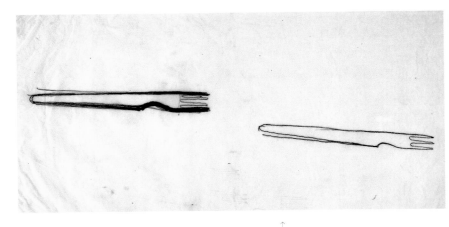

↑
Sketch for flatware, 1957. Like the door
handle, the flatware was intended to be an
extension of the hand. In this early sketch,
a curve at the head of the fork provided a
recess for the forefinger.

↓
Annotated blueprint for the Royal Hotel
glassware, c. 1959. Stemware for wine and
spirits was complemented by tumblers
for beer and water. The drawing contains
notations of model number and capacity
for each glass, and Jacobsen's own marks
record his adjustments to the profiles.

AJA flatware, 1957. The flatware for the hotel restaurant was stamped from steel sheets and plated with silver. In this selection from the service, Jacobsen's use of related forms is especially clear in the group of spoons and the salad servers at the upper left. At the bottom of the picture, services for lunch and dinner were distinguished by differences in size and subtle details. In spite of the care with which Jacobsen designed these implements, they were quickly taken out of use. Eventually, however, the service found an audience and is still produced in matte and polished stainless steel as the AJ service.

↖
Ashtray and candleholder, 1958.
Jacobsen's economy of form is evident
in this design of an asymmetrical bowl
that could contain ashes or tapers.

←
Condiment set, 1958. In addition to salt
and pepper, mustard is an important sea-
soning in Danish cuisine. The spherical
saltshaker and mustard pot were complemented by a conical pepper shaker.

→
Candleholder for three tapers, 1958.
The silver-plated candleholder typified
Jacobsen's approach to domestic objects.
A single piece served as the module
for extended arrangements and could
be stacked for compact storage.
The curved bridge between the spheres
reflected Jacobsen's fusion of rational
and organic forms.

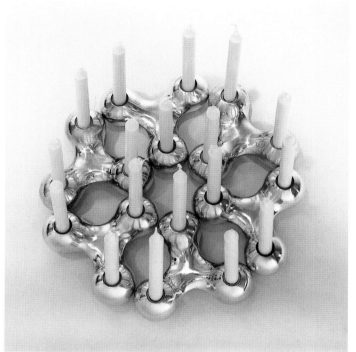

↓
Packaging design for S.O.F. caviar, 1959. Jacobsen designed the folding cardboard box using the three chimneys of his 1943 smokehouse as a logo for the fishery. In the display case, the lids of the glass jars repeated the abstract motif that combined geometric shapes with a reference to a specific landscape.

↓↓
Display case in the vestibule of the hotel restaurant. A freestanding display case, outfitted with tiny light bulbs, advertised the local roe, which guests could purchase in the hotel.

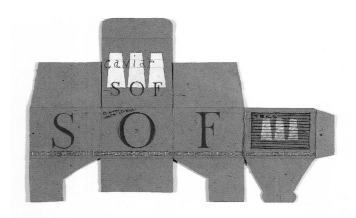

↑
Guest book of the Royal Hotel, 1960. The registry of notable visitors was bound in vellum and covered with a layer of gold lines that repeated the pattern of the curtain wall.

↑
Porcelain ashtrays, 1960. A series of ashtrays, turned at the Lyngby porcelain works outside of Copenhagen, were glazed in hues of blue, yellow, and white. In the restaurant and bar, where each table held an ashtray, the range of sizes and colors prevented an institutional effect.

→
Typeface for interior signs, 1959. The alphabet is an appropriate metaphor for Jacobsen's use of related forms to produce a complete vocabulary of forms and textures. This typeface, a modification of the standard Helvetica, was used for interior signage and provides further evidence of Jacobsen's desire to create a continuous, integrated experience.

Jacobsen also designed groups of silver hollowware, condiment sets, bud vases, ashtrays, and candleholders that continued the motif of curves established by the glasses and flatware. While most of these designs were graceful versions of familiar articles, the candleholder for three tapers realized Jacobsen's persistent goal of creating new type-forms. Composed of three spheres connected by a sculptural bridge, the candleholder could be used as a centerpiece or combined in an arrangement that created a lattice of direct and reflected light. When not in use, the units could be stacked for compact storage, a provision that recalled Kaare Klint's classes in furniture design. Like the flatware, the abstract candelabra revealed Jacobsen the applied artist at his most profound, radically reimagining a commonplace object and creating a new form that reflected the differences between modern life and traditional models. While he would continue to design hollowware in the 1960s, silver would be replaced by stainless steel, a shift in material that led toward objects of platonic geometry.

Jacobsen was devoted to improving the aesthetic quality of daily life, so almost no detail was so small as to escape his exacting standards and relentless creative energy. Throughout the SAS House, small touches, from typefaces to ashtrays, represented his attempt to ensure a consistent level of beauty and quality. The variety of these efforts, and of Jacobsen's protean talents in general, was encapsulated in a glass showcase on the second floor of the hotel. In the seating area leading to the restaurant, Jacobsen designed a six-sided vitrine to display the caviar that was served in the dining rooms and also available for sale to the public. He also designed the caviar's packaging, including on the side of the box an abstract emblem of the main plant, his own set of monumental chimneys completed for the Sjællands Oddes Fiskerøgeri (the Fish Smokehouse) in 1944.

The pursuit of a total design reflected Jacobsen's desire to join aesthetics and utility at every scale of experience. Rather than create an aesthetic monoculture in a single motif applied to a range of varied objects, Jacobsen made his most complete statement with constellations of different forms and materials that were united by a single aesthetic standard. In spite of his willingness to design virtually any object, he consciously searched for each design solution according to the logics of production and use. His pursuit of minimal form also represented a search for solutions in which shape and purpose were joined in a single body that was both radically new and functionally inevitable. He devoted such immense effort to the planning, design, and detailing of his buildings that he apparently could not bear to see their interiors degraded by furnishings and fixtures that were not produced with equal care or did not meet his standards of integrated form and simple beauty. At the SAS House, the scale and the prestige of the project allowed him to pursue his most complete artistic statement. In the years that followed, his work in the applied arts would shift from items for his buildings to designs for mass production..

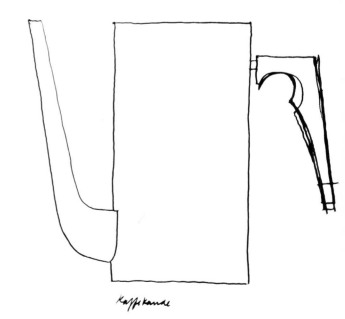

↓
Sketches for tea- and coffeepots, c. 1965.
Jacobsen's designs for a range of serving
vessels used the basic form of a cylinder
to relate objects of varied size and
function.

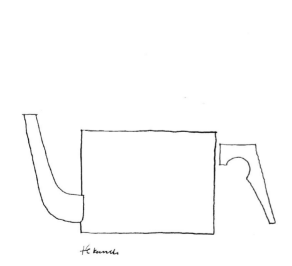

In the last decade of Jacobsen's life, his office was occupied with large-scale building projects at home and overseas, including laboratories and factories for Novo A/S, town halls and corporate buildings in Germany, and a new building for the National Bank of Denmark. In 1964, the office was restructured as Arne Jacobsen and Otto Weitling Associates, with Weitling, Jacobsen's employee since 1956, becoming a partner and assuming responsibility for a number of works, including the projects in Germany. In spite of this stream of large-scale commissions, Jacobsen continued to design household objects. By the early 1960s, the imprimatur of the architect on furnishings and household goods had become a powerful marketing tool, a development for which Jacobsen was largely responsible, and it offered him additional opportunities to realize his goal of inexpensive everyday goods. In contrast to the table settings for the Royal Hotel, which, apart from the steel flatware, had been produced through traditional craft practices, Jacobsen's later designs were intended for mass production. This shift in technique and audience was accompanied by an emphasis on platonic geometry and machined finishes. While his previous objects had been created for specific buildings and then marketed as products of mass appeal, the designs for industry were created as generic objects that could be used in any location.

Between 1964 and 1969, Jacobsen designed two product lines that broke new ground in his vocabulary and illuminated his changing relationship with industry. Cylinda was an attempt to produce a line of coffee and tea services, pitchers, and condiment sets that could be sold to a middle-class clientele. In 1964 Peter Holmblad, Jacobsen's stepson by Jonna Jacobsen, suggested that the architect design a new line of hollowware for the Stelton company, a manufacturer of stainless steel goods where Holmblad was employed as a salesman. In spite of the cachet that resulted from his involvement, Jacobsen hoped that the line would eventually be sold at modest outlets such as hardware stores. Like the commercial version of the AJA flatware, the new line jettisoned the ornament and associations of traditional silverware in favor of a machined product that reflected both the nature of the material and Jacobsen's own vision of sensuous utility.

Jacobsen and Holmblad settled on the cylinder as a form that would both suit a range of containers and provide a unified appearance to a table covered with objects of varied sizes and functions. The first designs were based on standard stainless steel pipes, cut to appropriate lengths, welded to bottoms, and fitted with a variety of lids, tops, and spouts. The closing of the tubes by machine was impractical, so the early products were instead rolled from steel sheets, hand-welded at the seam, and then ground and polished to achieve a pristine, machined appearance. While the use of standard pipe sizes was in keeping with a mass-produced product, the use of cylinders with set dimensions had additional benefits. By basing the form of the containers on an industrial product, as a sort of readymade, Jacobsen was able to bypass the initial design phase and concentrate on the details that were both a hallmark of his work and the threshold of experience for household objects.

←
Teapot with sugar and cream containers,
1967. While table tea and coffee services
have historically been made of fragile materials, the Cylinda line combines delicate
forms with the durable material of stainless steel.

→

Martini pitcher with coasters and spoons,
1967. The containers are distinguished by
meticulously crafted joints and edges that
reflect Jacobsen's attention to detail and
the precise workmanship made possible
by the hardness of the metal.

↓

Cylinda line, 1964–67. The basic premise
of the Cylinda line is clear in this group
of disparate items that are united by
a common material and a basic shape.
The original line comprised eighteen items
including, from left to right: creamer,
sugar pot, salt- and pepper shakers, water
pitcher, ice bucket, cocktail shaker, sauce
bowl, salad bowl, revolving ashtray,
martini pitcher, teapot, and coffeepot.

The initial group of products included a range of containers, including the pieces of traditional silver services, pots for coffee and tea, cream and sugar sets, and a tray for the group. Jacobsen also created cocktail shakers, ice buckets in three sizes, salt- and pepper shakers, a revolving ashtray, and a host of other vessels for the line. Beyond their common form, all of these items are distinguished by an attention to detail and a precise finish that are distinctly architectural. The connections between handles and vessels, the provision of small bearings to contain the lids of the coffee and tea pots, and the subtle drips that terminate the spouts and prevent liquids from running down the side all point to a careful consideration of function. At the same time, the durable stainless surfaces are resistant to denting, and while they are easily cleaned, they do acquire a patina with repeated use. Introduced in 1967, the Cylinda line was an almost immediate success. The resulting revenue allowed Holmblad to develop the equipment necessary to move the production from craft to industry.

Jacobsen's final design for industry was a series of plumbing fixtures for the manufacturer I.P. Lund Eftf. Following the success of the Cylinda line, the owner of the Lund company, Verner Overgaard, approached Jacobsen regarding a line of taps and faucets. Overgaard had perfected a new type of valve that would allow the fixtures to be built into the wall, but he felt that an aesthetic treatment was needed to distinguish his new line from traditional products. At the same time, the National Bank had progressed to the point that Jacobsen and Weitling were searching for plumbing fixtures. Jacobsen decided to design the line for use in the new building.

Although it would be introduced at the National Bank, the Vola range was intended from the start as a universal solution. Jacobsen's first decision was to treat the fittings as a modular system that could be integrated with standard European tile grids of ten and fifteen centimeters. The fixtures were mounted on cover plates, five centimeters high, that could be used with both sizes of tile. These consisted of a series of cylinders in descending sizes, from faucet to spout to handle. In addition to the wall-mounted fixtures, which included a handheld wand that served as a shower fixture, Jacobsen designed counter faucets for use in kitchens and commercial facilities. The components of the Vola line were made of brass, cast, rolled, or machined according to the individual component. Jacobsen had originally wanted the fixtures to have a brushed chrome finish, but it was technically unfeasible at the time. Instead they were coated in a baked-on epoxy polyester resin in two shades of gray selected by Jacobsen. Verner Overgaard renamed the company following the introduction of the line, and today the fixtures, greatly expanded and available in brushed chrome and a range of colors, are the sole product line of the Vola Company.

Rooted in the concern for the domestic interior that is a hallmark of Nordic culture, Jacobsen did not consider architecture and interior design separate disciplines. They were instead complementary activities that responded to different scales and requirements. With his concern for human comfort and a pre-

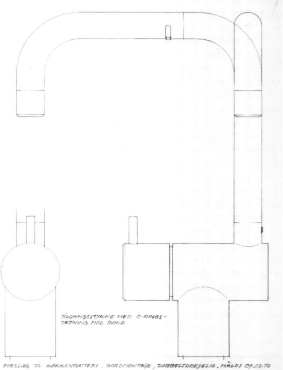

TILGANGSSTYKKE MED O-RINGS-
TÆTNING MOD BORD

FORSLAG TIL VÆRKSTEDSBATTERI. BORDMONTAGE, DOBBELTDREJELIG, MÅLR1 09.03.72

↑

National Bank of Denmark, Copenhagen,
1961–78. The Vola fixtures were introduced in the first phase of the bank building, completed shortly before Jacobsen's
death in 1971. On the workbenches of the
laboratory for dye quality, Vola faucets are
complemented by special chemical-
resistant handles and surface-mounted
nozzles for compressed air. Along the left
wall, fume hoods were built into the pear-
wood paneling.

←

Standing faucet from the Vola line. Jacobsen and his associate Teit Weylandt
designed a system of plumbing fixtures in
which all the elements were joined in a
single form.

ccupation with details and finishes, Jacobsen made designs dis-
nguished by a profound domesticity. The fact that so many of his
roducts, from the chairs and lighting fixtures of the 1950s to the
offee pots and bathroom faucets of the 1960s, remain in produc-
on today is a testament to his ability to combine beauty and
tility at every level. Despite the functionalist rhetoric that he
spoused until the end of his life, Jacobsen was fundamentally
evoted to aesthetics. In his mind, beauty was an essential quality,
s necessary as heat and ventilation.

↑
Arne Jacoben at the snack bar of the Roya
Hotel, c. 1960.

Dogged by controversy since its inception, Jacobsen's masterwork would survive only a handful of years before a slow process of dismemberment began. As early as 1963, Bent Salicath, editor of the applied arts journal *Dansk Kunsthaandværk*, was assailing the changes wrought by Alberto Kappenberger, the manager of the Royal Hotel from 1960 until 1981, in an article that referred to the building as a "fragile flower." Still, few changes were made to the SAS House prior to Jacobsen's death in 1971. In 1978, many of the guest rooms were renovated with new fabrics and colors that reflected the fashions of that decade. The winter garden was effectively dismantled in 1980 to enlarge the seating area for the snack bar, and in the next few years, the guest rooms were brightened by covering their wenge panels and boxes with a coat of white paint. The air terminal was renovated numerous times but remained open to travelers until mid-2002. It is now used for SAS staff offices, but its future is uncertain.

In 1988, the airline divested itself of its hotels, selling the Royal Hotel to a syndicate of individual investors and signing a management contract with an American hotel chain. With no one clearly in charge, the hotel deteriorated fairly quickly. In the early 1990s, the second floor was converted into conference rooms, the restaurant was relocated to the ground floor, and the interiors of the bar, lounges, and dining rooms were discarded. Between 1998 and 2001, the interiors of 274 guest rooms were discarded or sold to prescient furniture dealers and replaced with the kind of interiors one finds in any luxury hotel, in a variety of cities. That Room 606 was spared is a testament to the foresight of Kersi Porbunderwalla, the third manager of the Royal Hotel (1983–88) who, recognizing the cultural significance of Jacobsen's integrated work, chose a large double room that was still intact and declared it off-limits to future renovations. In addition, he assembled examples of the glass and silverwares made for the hotel and installed them in a wall-mounted vitrine in the sleeping area. Today, Room 606 is not protected by any of the legislation that has been so effective in preserving much older remnants of Denmark's cultural patrimony; its preservation is very much a matter of private benevolence.

Jacobsen was not a theorist and he never articulated a universal language of form. Instead, he worked in an intuitive manner, approaching each project, regardless of scale or material, as an opportunity to fuse his refined aesthetic with a specific function and new methods of construction. This empirical approach, and the protean nature of his work, have led Jacobsen to be largely neglected in the conventional histories of modern architecture. While his furnishings have become so ubiquitous, and so counterfeited, as to become anonymous, his buildings have been largely overlooked.

Jacobsen was one of the outstanding figures of twentieth-century architecture. At their very best, his buildings combine an unself-conscious humanism and a pragmatic aestheticism into singular monuments to the ability of architecture and design to enrich the lives of the inhabitants and ennoble the institutions of daily life. Taken as a whole, Jacobsen's work creates a modern aesthetic that reconciled the imperatives of large-scale building and mass production with the persistent human desires for variety, nuance, and sensual delight. The results were buildings that are still as functional and comfortable as the day they were completed.

Much of the persistent allure of Jacobsen's work – its oft-noted timeless quality – lies in the similarity of his construction techniques to today's methods. While considerable advances in building technology have been made since 1960, they are largely invisible, at the level of mechanical and electrical systems, insulation and sealants. The essential techniques of curtain wall framing, veneered woodwork, and finish carpentry have changed very little since Jacobsen's time. This similarity of technique and the power of his constructed landscapes highlight the relevance of his work now. The contemporary value of Jacobsen's work lies not only in the singular elegance of his forms, but also in his responses to the contradictory impulses of global and local cultures, advanced technology and traditional craft. In a career that spanned almost a half century and extended from the scale of the hand to the scale of the building, there are lessons for several lifetimes, most immediately our own.

→ Plan of Room 606, 1:40.

1 Hotel corridor
2 Toilet
3 Vestibule
4 Closets
5 Bathroom
6 Bedroom
7 3302 sofa
8 Dressing tables
9 Drop chair
10 FH 3515 table
11 Egg chair
12 Eklipta lamp above
13 Display case
14 Wool curtain
15 Window wall
16 Bedside table
17 Single beds

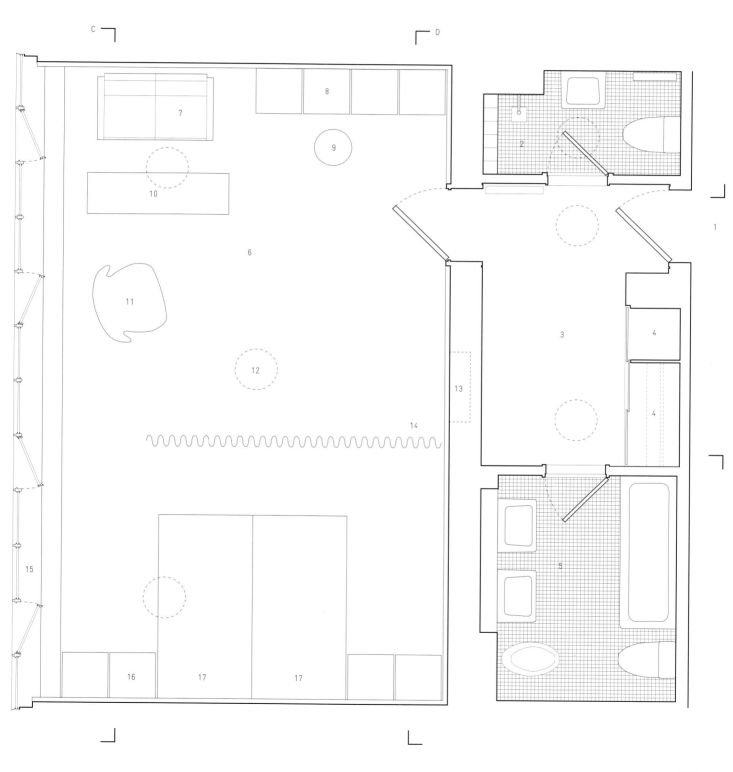

↓
Section A through bedroom and vestibule
facing west, 1:40.

↓↓
Section B through bedroom and vestibule
facing east (beds omitted for clarity), 1:4

1 Painted wallcovering
2 Window wall
3 Reading lamp
4 Wenge paneling
5 Painted wood baseboard
6 Dressing table
7 Mirror
8 Door to toilet
9 Painted wood paneling

1 Painted wallcovering
2 Window wall
3 Reading lamp
4 Wenge paneling
5 Bedside table
6 Painted wood baseboard
7 Painted wood paneling
8 Door to bathroom
9 Closet

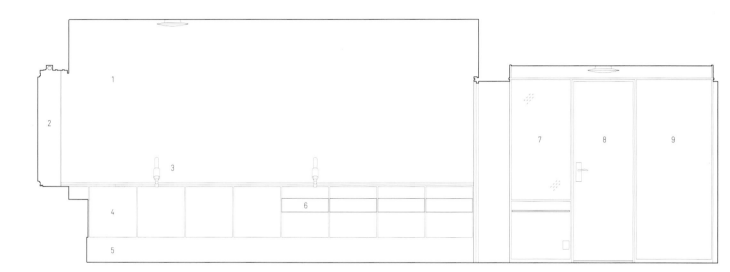

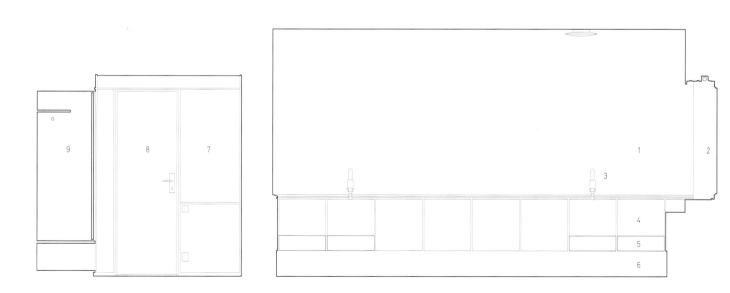

↓
Section C through bedroom facing
south, 1:40.

↓ ↓
Section D through bedroom facing
north, 1:40.

1 Eklipta ceiling lamp
2 Painted wood valence
3 Fixed window
4 Operable window
5 Wenge veneer
6 Painted wood baseboard
7 Air conditioner (added c. 1970)
8 Bedside table

1 Painted wallcovering
2 Dressing table
3 Wenge paneling
4 Painted wood baseboard
5 Door to vestibule
6 Display case (added 1987)
7 Wool curtain
8 Bedside table

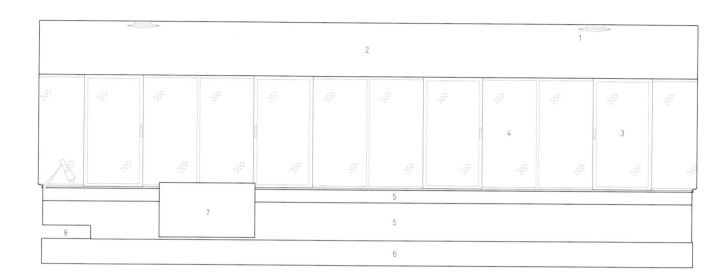

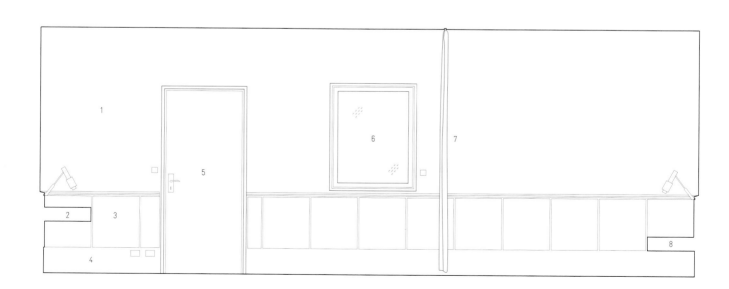

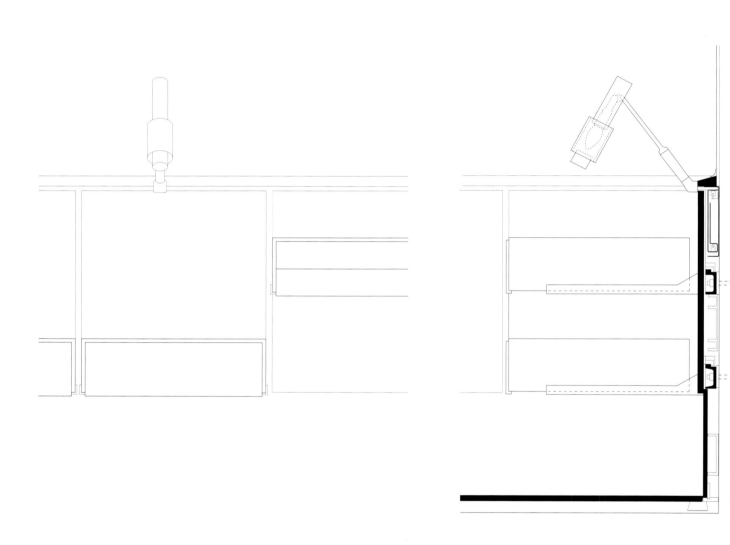

↑
Front view and section of the wood
paneling in Room 606, 1:10. The brackets
that supported the wall-hung boxes were
attached to steel channels bolted to the
concrete walls. Below the wood rail, an
accordionlike system of electrical wiring
provided power to the sliding lamps.

BOOKS

Faber, Tobias, *Arne Jacobsen*. Stuttgart, Germany: Verlag Gerd Hatje;
    London: Praeger; 1964.
Møller, Erik, and Kjeld Vindum, *Aarhus Town Hall*. Copenhagen: Arkitektens Forlag, 1991.
Pedersen, Johan, *Arkitekten Arne Jacobsen*. Copenhagen: Arkitektens Forlag, 1954.
Solaguren-Bescoa, Felix, *Arne Jacobsen: Works and Projects*. Barcelona:
    Gustavo Gili, 1991.
Thau, Carsten, and Kjeld Vindum, *Arne Jacobsen*. Copenhagen: Arkitektens Forlag, 1998.
Tøjner, Poul Erik, and Kjeld Vindum, *Arne Jacobsen: Architect and Designer*.
    Copenhagen: Danish Design Center, 1994.

PERIODICALS

"Armaturserie." *Arkitektur* 13, no. 3 (June 1969): 96–97.
"Atriumschule Munkegaard in Gentofte bei Kopenhagen."
    Bauen und Wohnen 11, no. 2 (February 1957): 65–72.
"Burohaus Jespersen og Son in Kopenhagen."
    Bauen und Wohnen 11, no. 6 (June 1957): 196–99.
"Court Design in Delightful Danish Elementary School, Vangede, Denmark."
    Architectural Forum 116, no. 6 (June 1957): 120–23.
"Denmark–The Massey Harris Establishment." *Architects' Yearbook* 6 (1955): 168–72.
"Fiskerøgeri ved Odden Havn." *Arkitekten Ugehæfte* 46 (1944): 185.
"Flats at Copenhagen." *Architectural Review* 108, no. 8 (August 1950): 123–26.
"Harby Skole, Fyn." *Arkitekten Maanedshæfte* 55, no. 10 (October 1953): 145–46.
"Haus eines Kaufmanns in Vedbaek, Dänemark." *Werk* 45, no. 6 (June 1958): 185–87.
Henriksen, Bård, "Arne Jacobsen and His Laminated Chairs."
    Scandinavian Journal of Design History 7 (1997): 7–28.
Hitchcock, Henry-Russell, "European Skyscrapers." *Zodiac* 9 (1961): 4–17.
"Hotel SAS Copenhague." *Arquitectura* 3, no. 25 (April 1961): 24–38.
"Houses near Copenhagen." *Architectural Review* 111, no. 2 (February 1952): 101–8.
"Hus i Vedbaek." *Arkitektur* 1, no. 6 (December 1957): 173–78.
"Hus på Parkovsvej." *Arkitektur* 6, no. 3 (June 1962): 85–89.
"Kontorbygning for A. Jespersen & Son." *Arkitektur* 2, no. 4 (August 1958): 109–14.
"Munkegaard School, Gentofte, Denmark."
    Architect and Building News 203 (14 May 1953): 574–75.
"Munkegårdsskolen i Gentofte." *Arkitektur* 1, no. 1 (February 1957): 1–11.
"Rækkehusbebyggelsen 'Søholm'." *Arkitekten Ugehæfte* 50 (1948): 65–67.
"Ratshus in Rödovre bei Kopenhagen."
    Bauen und Wohnen 10, no. 11 (November 1956): 401–8.
"Recent buildings." *Zodiac* 5 (1959): 44–53.
"Rødovre radhus." *Arkitekten Maanedshæfte* 58, no. 10 (October 1956): 153–68.
"Royal Hotel." *Arkitektur* 4, no. 6 (December 1960): 209–48.
"Royal Hotel, Copenhagen." *Architectural Design* 31, no. 1 (January 1961): 39–40.
"Das Royal-Hotel der Scandinavia Airlines System in Kopenhagen."
    Baukunst und Werkform 14, no. 13 (March 1961): 136–52.
"Royal SAS Hotel." *International Lighting Review* 12, no. 2 (February 1961): 42–51.
"St. Catherine's College, Oxford." *Architects' Journal* 140 (5 August 1964): 323–42.
"St. Catherine's College i Oxford." *Arkitektur* 9, no. 1 (February 1965): 1–40.
"SAS Air-Terminal." *Arkitektur* 3, no. 2 (April 1959): 45–54.
"SAS-Hotel und Air Terminal in Kopenhagen."
    Bauen und Wohnen 15, no. 3 (March 1961): 97–112.
"SAS-Hotellet in Kopenhagen." *Byggmastaren* 37 (4 October 1958): 208–9.
"School near Copenhagen." *Architect and Building News* 211 (4 April 1957): 436–45.

"Sea-Side Flats near Copenhagen."
    Architect and Building News 147 (24 July 1936): 104–6.
"Soholm Housing Estate near Copenhagen."
    Architect and Building News 202 (14 August 1952): 205–9.
"Sommerhus i Tisvilde." *Arkitektur* 1, no. 3 (June 1957): 184–85.
"Stellings Hus, Gammel Torv." *Arkitekten Maanedshæfte* 40, no. 9
    (September 1938): 125–32.
"Theatre and Restaurant, near Copenhagen."
    Architect and Building News 154 (10 June 1938): 299–303.
"To Boligbebyggelser–Atriumhuse ved Carlsminde."
    Arkitekten Ugehæfte 57 (February 1955): 93–96.
"Town Hall at Rødovre; Copenhagen, Denmark."
    Architects' Journal 125 (21 March 1957): 429–32.
"Town Hall at Søllerød." *Architectural Review* 101, no. 5 (May 1947): 173–76.
"Two Houses North of Copenhagen."
    Architect and Building News 203 (12 March 1953): 315–19.
"Tryckta Tyger av Arne Jacobsen."
    Form: Svenska Slöjdföreningens Tidskrift 3–4 (1944): 10–11.

Page numbers in *italic* refer to the illustrations

PHOTOGRAPHIC CREDITS

t=top, b=bottom, l=left, r=right, c=center

Avery Architectural and Fine Arts Library,
    Columbia University in the City of New York: p.204bl
Amy Barkow, photographer: pp.162b, 204br
Library of the Royal Danish Academy of Fine Arts;
    Arne Jacobsen, photographer: pp.8, 60bl&br, 166t, 213, 218
Bruun Rasmussen Auktioner: p.220t&cl
Dansk Møbelkunst; Maria Lassen/Ole Høstbo, photographers:
    pp.42bl, 152b, 185lt&lb, 206, 212, 216t
Dissing + Weitling Architects: p.91t, 194
Dissing + Weitling Architects; Adam Mørk, photographer: p.90t
Dissing + Weitling Architects; Mydtskov & Rønne, photographers. pp.234, 236lt&lc
The SAS Archive, The Royal Library, Copenhagen; Erik Hallstrøm, photographer:
    pp.14, 20–21, 22t, 100, 105tr&bl, 106b, 154lb, 182, 183t, 184t, 186–87t
Fritz Hansen Eftf.: p.220cr
Fritz Hansen Eftf.; Søren Nielsen photographer: p.236br
Fritz Hansen Eftf.; Aage Strüwing, photographer:
    pp.208t, 210bl, 219t&c, 220b, 230–31, 235, 236lb
The Library of the Royal Danish Academy of Fine Arts, Copenhagen;
    Jørgen Watz, reproduction photographer: pp.12, 16lt&b, 18, 32, 36–37, 42bcl, 44–46,
    54t, 59b, 70, 72, 78t&bl, 106t, 110–111, 113t, 126, 128b, 134t, 139t, 158, 160tl,
    162t, 163, 168, 174b, 176, 180–81, 188, 190, 204t, 210br, 219b, 224, 226, 248,
    252tl&b, 254r
Louis Poulsen A/S; Bent Ryberg, reproduction photographer: pp.34b, 96, 98b
Courtesy Royal Hotel; Paul Warchol reproduction photographer: p.68
Courtesy St Catherine's College, Oxford, England: p.60t
Courtesy Michael Sheridan:
    pp.10, 39–41, 50, 54b, 55t, 59t, 74t&r, 84t&r, 88t&r, 115c, 124t, 185r, 198t
Scanpix/Nordfoto; Børge Lassen, photographer: p.260
Reproduced by permission of Jørgen Strüwing; Aage Strüwing, photographer: pp.16r, 22b,
    30, 34t, 42t, 48, 51, 53, 56b, 57–58, 74b, 75–76, 78br, 80, 81, 84bl, 85–87, 88bl&br,
    90b, 91b, 98t, 102–4, 105br, 108, 112, 113b, 114, 115t&b, 116–18, 120–23, 124b,
    128t, 130–33, 134b, 135–36, 138, 139b, 146, 148, 150–151, 152t, 153, 154lt,
    154–57, 160tr, 164–65, 166b, 178, 183b, 184b, 186b, 192–93, 195–97, 198b, 208b,
    209, 210t, 214, 216b, 217, 222, 227–28, 232, 242bl&br, 244, 246, 249–51,
    252tr&cl&cr, 258t
The Swedish National Museum, Stockholm;
    Reproduction photographer, Erik Cornelius: p.160bl&br
Stelton A/S: pp.254l, 256
Tobias Jacobsen: p.52
Vola: p.258
Paul Warchol Photography; Paul Warchol, photographer:
    pp.26, 28, 38, 42bcr&br, 64, 66, 94, 97, 142, 144, 172, 174t, 202, 240, 242t,

All line drawings were redrafted by the author using original documents from the Library
of the Royal Danish Academy of Fine Arts.

his book is dedicated to William F. Sheridan and Richard A. Plunz

he project began in 1999 when I traveled through Scandinavia nder the auspices of a Norden Travel and Research Grant. The orden Grant is an annual prize that is administered by the Archiectural League of New York in commemoration of Deborah J. orden. Ms. Norden was an architect and arts administrator in New ork City and she devoted her career to advancing the civic arts as means to a better city. I am profoundly grateful to the Norden fam-y for their generosity in establishing the award program and I hope hat this book can contribute to the legacy of a remarkable woman.

It is no exaggeration to say that Room 606 would not have een possible without the extraordinary assistance of Jørgen trüwing and Claus M. Smidt. By allowing me repeated access to he collection of negatives taken by his father, Mr. Strüwing made possible for me to create a visual reconstruction of the SAS House nd illustrate the links between the various phases of Jacobsen's ork. In addition, I am thankful to Jette Strüwing for her hospitality nd friendship during my repeated visits to Denmark. As curator of he Architectural Drawings Collection at the Kunstakademiet, Mr. midt granted me the privilege of exploring Jacobsen's original rawings and watercolors. In this research, I was ably assisted by ørgen Watz, Dorrit Bergqvist, and most particularly, Søren Christiensen who displayed enormous enthusiasm and patience hroughout my extensive search.

Exploring Jacobsen's work in furniture and the applied arts s a complex task and necessarily requires the input of many ersons, companies, and institutions. I wish to thank Ida Præste-aard at Louis Poulsen A/S for access to the original drawings of Jacobsen's lamps. At Fritz Hansen A/S, Marianne Gulløv and Marlene Myhre made it possible for me to examine the scrapbooks nd archival materials that chronicle Jacobsen's long relationship vith the company. Charlotte Brøndum made new prints from the urniture negatives under difficult conditions, allowing me to add mages to the book at a fairly late date. Michael Von Essen of the Georg Jensen Museum and Peter Husted of Stelton A/S guided my esearch into Jacobsen's designs for the tabletop. Two curators of extiles, Charlotte Paludan at the Kunstindustrimuseet in Copen-hagen and Barbro Hofstadius at the Swedish National Museum in Stockholm, were instrumental in my understanding of the relation-ship between Jacobsen's textiles and his buildings. At the Royal Danish Library, Arne S. Andersen patiently assisted me in review-ing the negatives of Erik Hallstrøm, while Kjeld Kjeldsen and Tine Vindfeld at the Louisiana Museum of Art graciously granted me access to Jacobsen's own slides even as they were working on the major retrospective of Jacobsen's career. Ole Høstbo and Dorte Slot of Dansk Møbelkunst have been a constant source of advice and, along with Peter Beck of Bruun Rasmussen Auktioner, provided important images of rare furnishings and fixtures.

At the Royal Hotel, a succession of persons have aided me with access to Room 606, particularly Irene Mikkelsen, who arranged for my first stay in the room as well as Colin J. Seymour, Aileesh Carew, and Solveig Bertelsen. I am particularly grateful to Alberto Kappenberger for his correspondence and his recollections. Elsewhere in Copenhagen, Eric Messersmidt, Thomas Brinch, Carsten Thau, Kjeld Vindum, and Teit Weylandt provided friendship and sup-port. In New York, at a very early stage in this project, Lillian Hess, Philip Nobel, Andrea Monfried, and Pernille Pedersen helped me to envision this book with their enthusiasm and encouragement. Michael Rock and Sze Tsung Leong helped me to give the project dimension and depth. I am particularly grateful to Paul Warchol, who believed in this project when it was only an outline and pro-vided invaluable documentation of the last fragment of a master-work. Once the project was set in motion, Richard Solomon and the Graham Foundation for Advanced Studies in the Fine Arts provided support that was crucial in producing the document in its current form. At Phaidon, Valérie Vago-Laurer and Patrick Busse helped me distill an enormous mass of material into this testament to Jacobsen's work and ideas. Nico Schweizer of Mediadub worked tirelessly to create a graphic structure that reflects the scope of the book and incorporates a diverse array of images. I am grateful to you all.

Phaidon Press Limited
Regent's Wharf
All Saints Street
London N1 9PA

Phaidon Press Inc.
180 Varick Street
New York, NY 10014

www.phaidon.com

First published 2003
Reprinted in paperback 2010
© 2003 Phaidon Press Limited

ISBN 978 0 7148 6108 1

A CIP catalogue record for this book is available
from the British Library

Support for the author's research has been
provided by the Graham Foundation for Advanced
Studies in the Fine Arts.

Designed by Nico Schweizer
Printed in Hong Kong